For an Ontology
of Morals

FOR AN ONTOLOGY
OF MORALS:

A Critique
of Contemporary Ethical Theory

HENRY B. VEATCH

Northwestern University Press

Evanston 1971

Permission has been granted by the publisher to quote from Jean-Paul Sartre, *Being and Nothingness,* trans. Hazel E. Barnes, copyright 1956 by the Philosophical Library, Inc.

Henry B. Veatch is Professor of Philosophy at Northwestern University. He is the author of *Two Logics,* also published by Northwestern University Press.

FOR SAM AND TOM

CONTENTS

FOREWORD

To come flat out for an ontology of morals will surely strike many as smacking of impertinence, not to say reaction. For is not the precise import of the currently fashionable concerns in ethics with such things as the language of morals, or the phenomenology of morals, simply that anything like an ontology of morals has been effectively displaced—and hopefully may remain eternally displaced—from the serious councils of serious philosophers? For our part we cannot hope to conceal the fact that in this book we are indeed using "ontology" in just that invidious sense which has prompted nearly all contemporary writers on ethics, be they analysts or existentialists, to want to have nothing whatever to do with ontology. The word most certainly does connote something decidedly pre-Kantian, if not actually Wolffian, in character. And nowadays, to be pre-Kantian is almost like being prehistoric; while to be Wolffian is to be practically unspeakable!

Our response to such hostility is simply to offer no defense, but rather to come forward and submit humbly and with good grace to the certain fate of being considered prehistoric. But as to our being Wolffian, that, we do think, would be going too far! Still, supposing that we might be permitted further to set the stage for our own performance, why not frankly acknowledge that for anyone to take ethics as somehow presupposing an ontology is indeed to imply that moral and ethical distinctions—distinctions between good and bad, right and wrong, ought and ought not, etc.—are somehow grounded in the very being and nature of things? In this sense, a major thesis of our book is that moral and ethical distinctions cannot be rightly or adequately understood if they are regarded simply

ix

as matters of linguistic use, or as but so many ways in which upon occasion our experience comes to be structured and colored for us, or as mere aspects under which sometimes things inescapably present themselves to us, as contrasted with the ways in which these same things are in themselves, and quite apart from our talk about them or the phenomenal guise under which we come to experience them. Of course, as to whether this somewhat unfashionable thesis can be sustained in the succeeding chapters remains to be seen.

Meanwhile, while we are about the business of explanation and apology, not to say confession, we ought at least to advert to those devastating strictures which Richard Taylor has so effectively leveled against the entire enterprise of so-called meta-ethics in the preface to his recent book, *Good and Evil*. He begins with the scornful observation:

> One would search in vain in these pages for any discussion of the naturalistic fallacy, of whether "ought" implies "can," of the practical syllogism, or the other fastidious puzzles that have somehow come to be thought of in some circles as important to ethics. Also missing are appraisals of utilitarianism, deontologism, intuitionism, cognitivism, and the rest of the baggage of what has pretentiously come to be known as *metaethics*. And most of all, the currently favorite ploy of talking about "what we would say" about this or that minute situation and "what we mean" by this or that ethical term has been avoided here. These seem to me to be poor substitutes for what a wise man ought to think about things of human significance.[1]

To this we find it hard to respond with anything but "Bravo!" At the same time, the subtitle of the present book proclaims it to be no less than about meta-ethics, and the book itself is loaded with just such "baggage" as Taylor so heartily deplores. Nor is it free from frequent references to many of those "fastidious puzzles" which are the stock in trade of contemporary writers on ethics, and which Taylor would so summarily rule out altogether.

Our defense is that if contemporary meta-ethics is the exercise in fu-

1. Richard Taylor, *Good and Evil: A New Direction* (New York: Macmillan, 1970), p. xi.

tility which Taylor says that it is, then why not try to diagnose the ill and see just where it is that so great an undertaking could presumably have gone so wrong? Might it not just be that much of the futility of recent meta-ethics is due to its having so carelessly and so confidently turned its back on ontology? After all, Taylor is surely not unaware of the fact that among his distinguished predecessors who have occupied themselves with the question of good and evil, there was one—and he perhaps not the least distinguished—who did not hesitate to say in no uncertain terms that the end of ethics is not knowledge but action.[2] At the same time, for all of his insistence upon ethics being a practical science, Aristotle was hardly one to neglect the theoretical foundations of ethics.[3] True, he did not do so under any such heading as "meta-ethics," but rather under what his later editors came to label as "metaphysics." Accordingly, one is tempted to wonder whether the proper cure for the sickness of meta-ethics is not so much its abolition, as Taylor would recommend, but rather its rehabilitation—if not through metaphysics, that being not exactly fashionable these days, then why not through a meta-meta-ethics?

2. Aristotle *Nicomachean Ethics* Bk. II, chap. 2, lls. 1103b26–28.
3. This interpretation of Aristotle, it must be admitted, has been frequently challenged. In rebuttal, however, see the recent article by J. Owens, "The Ground of Ethical Universality in Aristotle," in *Man and World,* II, no. 2 (1969), 171–93.

ACKNOWLEDGMENTS

In any book such as this, which runs so decided a risk of being either scorned or ignored, one hesitates to make acknowledgment to anyone, lest he be immediately victimized through guilt by association. Nevertheless, my debt to the following is so great that I can but plead their innocence at the same time that I express my appreciation. Miss Marjorie Clay was kind enough to read an entire first draft of the book, making numerous suggestions for stylistic improvements, as well as carefully checking my careless references and supplying still other references which I had simply omitted. Professor Stanley Rosen was as charitable as he was wise in recommending a thorough reworking of the whole book—advice which I did not act on sufficiently. Also, my friend and former colleague, Professor M. S. Gram, took both me and my typescript firmly in hand, inveighing against both my philosophical errors and my stylistic indiscretions. I listened carefully and rewrote faithfully, but still not to his satisfaction, as will be only too apparent from the production which follows.

Once again to the staff of the Northwestern University Press, and particularly to Mrs. Joy Neuman, I want to express my continuing thanks for their never-failing tact, skill, and determination in striving so valiantly to make a silk purse out of a sow's ear.

For an Ontology
of Morals

I

SETTING FOR
A STRUCTURAL HISTORY

~~~~~~

Could it be that contemporary ethics has just about reached a dead end? Not that such a thing has really dawned on the philosophers and ethical writers concerned, for the presses continue to pour forth streams of articles and books on ethics, written by both high- and low-placed professors, particularly among the linguistic analysts, but to a lesser extent among the existential phenomenologists as well. It is as though these philosophers had not yet begun to realize that their continued and by now uncritical reliance upon certain kinds of philosophical method—notably that of linguistic analysis on the one hand and of phenomenology on the other— had so hemmed them in and straitened them in their consideration of ethical questions that in their capacity as moral philosophers they seem not to have room for maneuver any more and may even, to change the metaphor, be well-nigh at the end of their rope.

It is not merely a case where what the professors of ethics have to say appears no longer relevant to the countless moral and ethical issues that have suddenly exploded in the faces of today's youth—issues of sex, of drugs, of war and peace, of pollution, of the military-industrial complex, etc. No, one suspects that, more fundamentally, it is a case of a latter-day scholasticism which does not sense its own limitations, and which, entrenched as it is academically, is still able to keep going through the same old motions, even though these motions no longer get anywhere and have thus largely lost their one-time point and purpose.

Nevertheless, in order to confirm and diagnose these, if not unsuspected, then still largely unrecognized, ills of contemporary ethics, let us undertake to sketch out a bit of what Bergmann might call the "structural history"[1] of recent ethics and ethical theory, as these have been purveyed on the one hand by the analysts and on the other hand by the existentialists and existential phenomenologists. For different as are the methods and ways of doing philosophy on the part of these two schools, it is interesting to observe how in matters of ethics they might both be said to have started out by reacting against much the same thing, and how eventually, having overcome a similar opposition, they have now both come to pursue their respective philosophical methods to much the same end—which, alas, might be suspected of being something of a dead end!

Natural-Law Ethics as a Foil

And what was it that these two schools began by reacting against? No sooner, however, is this question put than immediately we shall be told that there was no one school or type of ethics that either analysts or existentialists could be said to have set themselves against—at least not in any univocal sense. Thus, while G. E. Moore began his philosophical career by defending realism as over against idealism, in ethics his prime and initial target might be said to have been what he chose to call "naturalism"; and naturalism, so conceived, was hardly reducible simply to idealism. And Kierkegaard did indeed fulminate against Hegel, but could it properly be said that it was solely and exclusively the ethical im-

---

1. To my knowledge Bergmann nowhere presents an extended treatment of his notion of structural history, but it has become a commonplace among members of his school. What Bergmann presumably means by it is simply that the various philosophical insights and proposals of different philosophers often involve structural implications and requirements, of which the authors themselves may not always be too clearly aware, and which sometimes do not emerge altogether unequivocally even in the subsequent actual history of philosophy. In many ways, such an implied contrast between an interpretive, structural history of philosophy and a literal, step-by-step history is reminiscent of some of Gilson's suggestions as to the point and purpose of the history of philosophy (see E. Gilson, *The Unity of Philosophical Experience* [New York: Scribner's, 1937]).

port of Hegelianism that he was concerned about? On the contrary, Kierkegaard's satire was aimed, among other things, directly at the morals and ethics of the type that he called that of "the serious man," a type that comes in for continuing castigation at the hands of such latter-day existentialists as Sartre and Simone de Beauvoir. Yet "the serious man" in his moral practice and behavior exemplifies more than the narrowly idealistic or Hegelian type of ethics that drew Kierkegaard's ire; as an image, it might equally well be said to exemplify precisely that form of naturalism or objectivism in ethics that Moore held to be not so much morally suspect as downright logically fallacious.

Still, for all of the complexions and complexities of the recent history of ethical theory, there is really no need to lose sight of the woods for the trees. Perhaps one way to keep the woods properly in sight is to consider a single traditional type of ethical theory and to let it serve as a foil against which the parallel concerns in ethics, whether analytic or existentialist, can be set forth in illuminating contrast. Our choice for such a foil is none other than the ancient and once honorable theory of so-called natural-law ethics. This is not to say that G. E. Moore or any of the other analysts, to say nothing of Kierkegaard or any of the later existentialists, thought of themselves as reacting consciously and specifically against every or even any natural-law theories of ethics. Yet a little reflection should suffice to show that quite a number of the basic structural features of contemporary ethical theories can be understood precisely in terms of their diametrical opposition to various corresponding structural features of natural-law ethics.[2]

Just what, though, is one to understand by the notion of a natural-law

2. It must not be inferred from this somewhat sweeping statement that we are assuming that in the entire history of Western thought there has been but a single, univocal tradition of natural-law ethics. To be convinced of the contrary, one has only to consult even so elementary, but nonetheless excellent, historical account of natural law as that given in D'Entrèves' little book, *Natural Law* (London: Hutchinson's University Library, 1951). Nevertheless, for all of the ambiguities and complications both in the concept and in the tradition of natural law, we hope in the pages that immediately follow to be able to focus upon a single more or less dominant strain in the natural-law tradition that should be sufficiently precise and univocal to allow of its use as a foil to point up the contrast with various contemporary ethical theories.

ethics? The basic idea is that just as there are laws in accordance with which things occur or changes take place in the natural world, which may therefore be said to determine the behavior and operations of the various things in nature, so also there are laws—natural laws—that determine what the natural and proper behavior for a human being is. Thus Hooker characterizes law in general as:

> That which doth assign unto each thing the kind, that which doth moderate the force and power, that which doth appoint the form and measure of working, the same we term a *Law*.[3]

At first, such explanations and such quotations as to the notion of natural law may seem more of a hindrance than a help. For one thing, when Hooker speaks of "assigning," "moderating," and "appointing," one may well feel that although he may have been trying to tell us what law is, he is in fact succeeding only in distracting our attention from the meaning of law to what he doubtless hoped would be of more primary concern to us, namely, God the lawgiver. And, naturally, in this day and age the idea of God is nothing if not anathema.

Moreover, any talk about "laws of nature" suggests to us nothing if not "scientific laws." And scientific laws have come to be understood as but so many "generalizations," which, "whether of strictly universal or of statistical form, purport to express regular connections among directly observable phenomena."[4] How, though, can such mere generalizations from constant conjunctions that have been simply observed to hold between various phenomena in nature even be imagined to "appoint the form and measure of working" or to "determine the behavior of the various things in nature"? In other words, the modern notion of natural law, while it may well be taken to be expressive of regularities in nature, is certainly not to be thought of as in any way regulative of what happens

---

3. Richard Hooker, *Of the Laws of Ecclesiastical Polity*, Book I, ed. Rev. John Keble (Oxford: The University Press, 1836), Vol. I, sect. 2, p. 249.

4. This brief quotation is taken from Hempel's well-known paper, "The Theoretician's Dilemma." It is reprinted in Dudley Shapere, *Philosophical Problems of Natural Science* (New York: Macmillan, 1965), p. 35.

in nature. Accordingly, in what we have quoted from Hooker, as well as in our own attempts at explicating the notion of "natural law," it would seem that we may not so much have clarified things as simply gone counter to what every right-thinking and scientifically-instructed man of today would understand by such notions as "natural laws" or "laws of nature."

So be it. And yet what we propose to do is to try to make a virtue, if not of our own necessity, then at least of our own wrongheadedness. We will be frank to admit that one can never properly appreciate either the character or the claims of a natural-law type of ethics if one invokes the modern scientific notion of natural law by way of explanation. Recourse must be had to an older notion than that which has now come to be in fashion among contemporary scientists and philosophers of science. Nevertheless, what is old-fashioned and out of place in the context of contemporary science need not be old-fashioned and out of place generally, particularly if our concern is one of learning to be not just scientists but human beings as well. And surely, in that everyday world of common-sense existence in which, as human beings, and for all of our scientific sophistication, we can hardly cease to live and move and have our being, we do indeed find ourselves constantly invoking an older and even a decidedly common-sense notion of "nature" and of "natural law." For don't we all recognize that a rose is different from an eggplant, and a man from a mouse, and hydrogen from manganese? To recognize such differences in things is surely to recognize that they behave differently: one doesn't expect of a man quite the same things that one does of a mouse, and vice versa. Moreover, the reason our expectations thus differ as to what various types of things or entities will do, or how they will act and react, is simply that they just are different kinds of things. They have different "natures," as one might say, using the old-fashioned terminology.

Moreover, it is in virtue of a thing's nature—i.e., of its being the kind of thing that it is—that it acts and behaves in the way it does. Is it not also in virtue of a thing's nature that we often consider ourselves able to judge what that thing might be or could be, but perhaps isn't? A plant, for example, may be seen to be underdeveloped or stunted in its growth. A bird with an injured wing is quite obviously not able to fly as well as others of the same species. And even in physical nature do we not sometimes speak as though the action, say, of some catalytic agent had been inhibited or interfered with, with the result that the anticipated change just did not come off or failed to complete itself? And so it is that a thing's nature may be thought of as being not merely that in virtue of which the thing acts or behaves in the way it does, but also as a sort of standard in terms of which we judge whether the thing's action or behavior is all that it might have been or could have been. Of course, one scarcely dares entertain any notions like that of "end" or "telos" in connection with natural processes, our present-day enlightenment being such that the light must surely blind us totally if we even so much as allow words like "end" or "goal" or "final cause" to cross our lips. Still, at the risk of such darkness at noonday we must accede at least to a certain initial plausibility of our understanding "natural law" as being not just the law of a thing's own nature but also the law which, as Hooker says, even "doth appoint the form and measure of [that thing's] working." [5]

So be it, then, that the notion of "natural law" as here used does, indeed, depart quite markedly from the contemporary scientific understanding of "nature" and of "law." Of course, it still remains for us to show just what the fact or reality of such natural laws must involve ontologically.[6] It further remains for us to show whether and how such ontologically grounded natural laws can have any moral or ethical import. For the present, though, must it not be acknowledged that at least the notion of

5. The kind of contrast that we have been implying, not merely between two different conceptions of natural law, but between two radically different ways of thinking, and even ways of being, we have sought to develop at greater length in our book, *Two Logics: The Conflict between Classical and Neo-Analytic Philosophy* (Evanston: Northwestern University Press, 1969).

6. Whether it is ultimately essential to the notion of law as here presented that it proceed from some divine lawgiver is really of no moment, so far as the basic argument of a natural-law ethic is concerned. After all, to take an analogous case, it may well be that the Aristotelian's notion of causation is of a sort to imply that ordinary natural causes must ultimately imply a first cause or unmoved mover. And yet this does not mean that such natural causes may not be examined and studied in "physics" without one's necessarily having to refer to such first causes or unmoved movers as they must ultimately all depend upon. Needless to say, this last remark is made without prejudice to Aristotle's inclusion of Books VII and VIII in his own *Physics*.

8

natural laws in this sense is a viable one, and perhaps even an indispensable one?

To return, then, to our story, let us consider briefly how Aquinas undertakes to elaborate still further this same general notion of law in terms of a "rule and measure of actions" (*quaedam regula et mensura actuum*)[7]— i.e., a rule and measure of how things act, determining, as it were, the distinctive character and regularity of their behavior. These notions of a rule or measure of a thing's action or behavior, in turn, imply for Aquinas the additional notions of an actual prescribing (*praecipere et prohibere*) of such behavior, and even a commanding (*imperare*) of it. Aquinas may be made to sound very much *à la mode* even in the present day, if one will but take the trouble to point the obvious moral that is here suggested —namely, that St. Thomas Aquinas appears to be well aware of what it is currently fashionable to call the "prescriptive" and "imperatival" character of all law.

Still, it is at this juncture that Aquinas' unpacking of the notion of law takes what to many would appear to be a very odd turn indeed. For as he sees it, the fact that all laws and norms have thus a prescriptive, imperatival character by no means implies that such laws and norms must be only convention—of νόμος, that is to say, and not of φύσις. Quite the contrary, man-made or humanly instituted, in the sense of being mere matter of commands and imperatives, he insists, are an affair of reason (*imperare est rationis*).[8] This does not merely mean that reason happens to be the one faculty which, in some agreed-upon psychological division of labor, is empowered to issue commands. Rather it means that no commands ever are or even can be issued by reason, save insofar as that which is so commanded should itself appear reasonable or should commend itself to reason. And what could thus commend itself to reason, unless it is recognizable as something that really and in fact ought to be done? That is to say, its very worth or excellence or obligatory character must be something that itself actually exists in nature.[9]

7. *Summa Theologiae* I–II. 90. 1.
8. *Ibid.*
9. This doubtless needs qualification in view of St. Thomas' recognition that in addition to eternal law and natural law there is also human law, which is simply a man-made law and hence not a law that could properly be said to "exist in nature."

9

In other words, for laws—and more generally still for moral standards and values—to be reasonable or to be in some sense or other rationally justifiable and defensible, rather than merely arbitrary, implies, on the natural-law theory, not just an ethical doctrine but an ontological doctrine as well. The worthwhileness or obligatoriness of things is actually there in things; it is no less a real feature of things than is, say, their being subject to change, or their being intelligible, or their having quantitative dimensions, or their being caught up in a causal order or what not. "Oughts" and "ought nots," "rights" and "wrongs," the "good" and the "bad"—these all have to be embedded right in the very nature of things.[10] Otherwise, how could they ever come to be discovered or recognized by reason? Reason could not possibly command or prescribe something as being required or obligatory or binding or incumbent upon us unless it were recognized as being really so in fact and in nature. It is this, indeed, that is the radical sense of a law's being said to be "natural."[11] Thus as Hooker phrases it in his inimitable Elizabethan English, "And the law of reason or human nature is that which men by discourse of natural reason have rightly found out themselves to be all for ever bound unto in their actions."[12]

But isn't this simply incredible, this notion of a natural-law ontology implied by a natural-law ethics, according to which so-called rules or

---

At the same time, St. Thomas is careful to point out that even such man-made law, if it is to be properly law at all, must be "derived from" natural law, either in the manner of conclusions derived from premises, or in the manner of determinations of more general principles (*determinationes quaedam aliquorum communium*). *Ibid.*, I–II. 95. 2.

10. Once again, a certain qualification is needed with respect to the second or privative member of each of the foregoing pairs. As is well known, Aquinas treats evil as being a privation of good (*Malum . . . non est aliquid, sed est ipsa privatio alicuius particularis boni*). See *De Malo*, I, 1. Moreover, privations are not, strictly speaking, *entia* at all and do not posit anything *in re*. See *De Ente et Essentia*, chap. 1.

11. Although the fact that a law might be "natural" in just this sense is implicit in Aquinas, it is not, strictly speaking, in this sense that he understands the term *lex naturalis*. Rather, natural law is to be understood primarily as simply that sharing in the eternal law by human beings in their capacity as rational animals. See *Summa Theologiae* I–II. 91. 2.

12. Hooker, *Laws of Ecclesiastical Polity*, pp. 290–91.

measures, prescriptions and requirements, standards of value and obligations are all a part of the very nature of things? Impossible!

Reasons in Ethics
as Implying an Ontology of Morals

Unhappily, there is not much that we can do just at present either to alleviate the incredibility or to remove the seeming fantasy. All of this must wait until later, when we hope to have brought our argument to the place where we shall finally be able to spell out in some detail just what the specific ontological features must be of such seemingly odd entities as laws, norms, values, obligations, and so on.

Still, it would seem that we ought to do at least a little better, even at this early stage, than merely to put off objectors with promissory notes. For even admitting that there is not much that we can do just now by way of showing how such things as rules and measures of actions can actually exist in reality and *in rerum natura,* is there not perhaps something that might be done by way of showing at least that it is possible? Already, we have hinted at such a thing in suggesting that, so far as the natural-law moralists were concerned, it was apparently taken for granted that if there were any properly rational grounds for our judgments as to good and bad or right and wrong, then these must imply real grounds or grounds in fact for such judgments. In other words, a rational basis for ethics seems to have been taken to entail an ontological basis. Is there, though, any warrant for such an assumption?

Now it almost goes without saying that, so far as contemporary ethical and meta-ethical literature is concerned, much is made of the fact that it is proper both to ask for and to give reasons for moral judgments and value judgments. Moreover, it is not uncommon, in the same connection, to point up a certain contrast between situations in which reasons are relevant in explanation of human actions as over against situations in which only causes and not reasons are relevant in the explanation of various natural events or happenings. Thus if the boat I am in gets caught in the trough of the waves and capsizes, and I suddenly find myself in the water, it is hardly appropriate to ask me for my reasons for being where I am. On the other hand, that there are at the same time causes of my present unhappy predicament, as opposed to reasons for it, is only too obvious: the boat turned over!

Now contrast with the foregoing situation one in which I deliberately throw myself overboard; then the question of reasons for my doing what I did immediately becomes relevant: was it because I wanted to take a swim, to save a friend from drowning, to manifest an *acte gratuit,* or what? In other words, just what was my reason for doing such a thing?

It should also be noted that the very logic of this business of reason-giving seems always to involve sooner or later an appeal to what the person in question considers to be right or worthwhile or good or obligatory or what not.[13] Nor is this surprising, for if an action, as contrasted with a mere natural event or occurrence, is something of our own, something that we do of our own choice and volition, then our reasons for so doing must ultimately reduce to our conviction that for us so to act must have something to recommend it, or have some value attached to it, or be something that we feel under some obligation to do.

Having pointed up the difference between giving reasons for our actions, as over against adducing causes for mere natural occurrences, let us turn to a consideration of a certain similarity between the two activities, at least in regard to what they would both seem to presuppose in the way of ontological commitment. Thus, so far as causes are concerned, is it not the case that for anyone to suppose x to be the cause of y is to suppose that x is a real cause—that is, that in the very nature of things causes are operative and thus have a certain ontological status, whatever the exact nature and character of that status may be? In fact, to put the point crudely: if I am convinced that there is no such thing as $x,$ and that x does not exist at all, then I certainly cannot speak with either honesty or conviction of x's being the cause of $y.$ And, even more generally, if I am convinced that causes just do not exist and have no ontological status of

13. We certainly do not wish to imply that these various standards that are appealed to in our reason-giving all come down to the same thing or make for reasons of the same kind. Nevertheless, for the point which we are trying to make in this present context, such differences as there may be between what are sometimes called teleological ethics and deontological ethics are hardly relevant.

any kind, then my use of the language of causation can hardly turn out to be anything other than dishonest or impossible.

And so, *mutatis mutandis,* would it also seem to be with reasons. For suppose that my reason for jumping out of the boat and into the water was in order to save a friend from drowning, does not the very fact that such was indeed my reason for so acting imply that I consider such behavior on my part to be in some sense or other the right thing to do, or a good thing to do, or something that I am under an obligation to do? Moreover, if I do indeed consider this to be the right thing to do, or something that it is my duty to do, does not this imply, in turn—analogously to our earlier causal example—that I regard such action as something that is really right or obligatory? Indeed, suppose that I did not so regard it, suppose that I were convinced that for me to try to save my friend in such circumstances just did not have any rightness about it at all, or was not anything that was really binding upon me, then it would scarcely seem that I could in honesty have given that as my reason for jumping overboard into the water. Even more generally, when it comes to giving reasons, just as with adducing causes, it would seem that if I am thoroughly convinced that nothing on the order of the beneficial or the worthwhile or the right has any ontological status of any kind and simply does not exist at all, then I cannot either in honesty or in strict logic ever presume to give reasons for any of my actions.

With this, though, may we not simply add a Q.E.D. so far as the ontology of natural law and more generally the ontological basis of morals and ethics are concerned? For if even contemporary ethical thinkers tend to stress the reasoned character of moral and ethical judgments, and if the mere fact that reasons can be given in ethics implies that ethics must therefore have a basis in fact and in nature, then there would appear to be no escaping the conclusion that not just a natural-law ethics but any ethics must carry with it either implicitly or explicitly a commitment to no less than an ontology of morals. And so, Q.E.D.! [14]

14. It may be hoped that the irony of this paragraph, with its breezy Q.E.D., will not be lost on the reader. For we should be the first to acknowledge that in many ways it would not be far wrong to say that the very question which contemporary ethical theorists, whether analysts or existentialists, are trying to raise is whether the

Analysts and Existentialists

in Opposition to Natural Law

Whatever one may think of this somewhat hasty, not to say ad hoc, demonstration that we have just put forward to show at least the prima facie possibility that norms, laws, rules, and measures of actions may indeed be natural—i.e., that they not only may but must have no less than an ontological status in fact and in reality—let him be at once reassured that no self-respecting contemporary thinker would give even so much as a snap of the fingers for this "demonstration." For, as we have already suggested, any ethics which pretends that distinctions between right and wrong, good and bad, etc., have a status in nature will be simply rejected out of hand by practically any and all contemporary moral philosophers, whether from the analytic camp or from that of the existential phenomenologists. Almost to a man these thinkers will protest that moral norms and moral laws just aren't to be thought of as having any such ontological status in the natural world at all. Thus, scarcely any ethical theory but a natural-law ethics could serve quite so well as a foil to bring out the salient and contrasting features of those contemporary ethical theories that currently strut and fret their hour upon the philosophic stage.

Take the analysts, for example. Doubtless, none of them would object if we were to cite as the *locus classicus* of their skepticism in regard to

•

---

reasoned character of ethical judgments need in any way imply or presuppose an ontological basis for such judgments. Accordingly, when we come along in our cavalier way and jauntily argue that if such things as moral distinctions and values generally have no ontological status in nature then our moral and value judgments cannot possibly be reasoned judgments at all, this only serves to beg the question, not meet it.

Granted! Still, it cannot be denied that there is at least a prima facie case for the more or less common-sense view that for a conclusion to be logically or rationally grounded there must somehow be real grounds in nature or in the world for the fact or facts that are being asserted in the conclusion. It is, therefore, this prima facie case that we should like to try to present in this first chapter; in subsequent chapters we will develop first the counter-case, and then, finally and hopefully, the rebuttal of this counter-case.

anything like natural norms and natural laws that famous passage from Hume's *Treatise* about willful murder:

> But can there be any difficulty in proving, that vice and virtue are not matters of fact, whose existence we can infer by reason. Take any action allow'd to be vicious: Wilful murder, for instance. Examine it in all lights, and see if you can find that matter of fact, or real existence, which you call *vice*. In which-ever way you take it, you find only certain passions, motives, volitions and thoughts. There is no other matter of fact in the case. The vice entirely escapes you, as long as you consider the object. You never can find it, till you turn your reflexion into your own breast, and find a sentiment of disapprobation, which arises in you, towards this action. Here is a matter of fact; but 'tis the object of feeling, not of reason. It lies in yourself, not in the object. So that when you pronounce any action or character to be vicious, you mean nothing, but that from the constitution of your nature you have a feeling or sentiment of blame from the contemplation of it. Vice and virtue, therefore, may be compar'd to sounds, colours, heat and cold, which, according to modern philosophy, are not qualities in objects, but perceptions in the mind.[15]

What could be more decisive than this: not just virtue and vice, but moral distinctions generally have no ontological status in the world of nature at all. Exit natural law!

Moreover, so far as the existentialists are concerned, one might say that the *locus classicus* of their repudiation of any and all forms of what might be called objectivism in ethics is precisely that passage in Kierkegaard which we adverted to earlier and in which he undertakes to satirize "the serious man." Note, though, that Kierkegaard's attack is somewhat differently directed than is Hume's. For Kierkegaard it isn't just that there are no natural laws or natural norms which are capable of being known by reason, but rather that, if there were such, they would be irrelevant and even corrupting so far as the human moral agent is concerned.

> The serious man continues: If he were able to obtain certainty with respect to such a good, so as to know that it is really there, he would

15. David Hume, *A Treatise of Human Nature*, ed. L. A. Selby-Bigge (Oxford: Clarendon Press, 1888), pp. 468–69.

venture everything for its sake. The serious man speaks like a wag; it is clear enough that he wishes to make fools of us like the raw recruit who takes a run in preparation for jumping into the water, and actually takes the run,—but gives the leap a go-by. When the certainty is there he will venture all. But what then does it mean to venture? A venture is the precise correlative of an uncertainty; when the certainty is there the venture becomes impossible. If your serious man requires the definite certainty that he seeks, he will be unable to venture all; for even if he does not get certainty, our serious man says in all earnest that he refuses to risk anything, since that would be madness. In this way the venture of our serious man becomes merely a false alarm. If what I hope to gain by venturing is itself certain, I do not risk or venture, but make an exchange. Thus in giving an apple for a pear, I run no risk if I hold the pear in my hand while making the exchange.[16]

Apparently, then, Kierkegaard has no more use for natural law than does Hume. For whereas Hume simply says there is no evidence of such a thing, Kierkegaard scornfully suggests that even if there were a natural law, of what possible good could it be, at least for ethics?

Accordingly, let these quotations from Hume and from Kierkegaard suffice for the time being as a clear indication of how nearly all of contemporary ethics, whether of the analytic or of the existentialist variety, may be seen to represent a sharp, as well as a sustained, reaction against anything smacking of a natural-law type of ethics. Still, the matter can scarcely be allowed to rest just here, for no sooner does any moral philosopher, ancient or modern, reject what we have somewhat awkwardly termed the ontology of natural law—that is, an objective status in nature for things like norms, standards, values, laws, etc.—than he is in danger of having to recognize that ethics, having no objective basis in fact, has no rational basis either. For have we not just seen how the natural-law moralists took it almost as a matter of course that if a moral standard or prescription is to be adjudged reasonable and not arbitrary, then it must have some sort of rational basis? But a rational basis for a prescribed law or standard must surely mean a real basis or a basis in nature.

Indeed, even Hume, if we consider the opening sentence of the above-

16. S. Kierkegaard, *Concluding Unscientific Postscript,* trans. D. Swenson and W. Lowrie (Princeton, N. J.: Princeton University Press, 1941), p. 380.

quoted passage, would appear to take it as evident that if vice and virtue can be shown not to be matters of fact, then their existence can scarcely be inferred by reason. By contraposition, this would surely imply that whatever can be determined by reason to be either right or wrong must be really right or wrong, or right or wrong in fact and as a matter of fact. In short, the principle is clear: take away the real or ontological ground for the rightness or wrongness of an action, and there will no longer seem to be any proper *reason* for anyone's holding it to be right or wrong. And without reasons for our moral judgments, we must acknowledge that such judgments are quite arbitrary. As Stanley Rosen has so tellingly put it at the very beginning of his book on nihilism:

> Nietzsche defines nihilism as the situation which obtains when "everything is permitted." If everything is permitted, then it makes no difference what we do, and so nothing is worth anything. We can, of course, attribute value by an act of arbitrary resolution, but such an act proceeds *ex nihilo* or defines its significance by a spontaneous assertion which can be negated with equal justification. More specifically, there is in such a case no justification for choosing either the value originally posited or its negation, and the speech of "justification" is indistinguishable from silence. For those who are not gods, recourse to a creation *ex nihilo* . . . reduces reason to nonsense by equating the sense or significance of speech with silence.[17]

Such words, though, could well be a bitter dose for many today who consider themselves moral philosophers. For what Rosen is saying amounts to this: if there can in principle be no proper reasons or no sort of rational basis for our moral and ethical judgments, then there can be no such thing as morals or ethics at all. Accordingly, contemporary moral philosophers tend to find themselves caught in a kind of dilemma. In fact, our reading of the structural history of recent ethical theory seems to indicate that this history is in very truth the chronicle of repeated and progressive attempts to break out of this dilemma. On the one hand, both the analysts and the existentialists appear to be in agreement in their determi-

17. Stanley Rosen, *Nihilism: A Philosophical Essay* (New Haven: Yale University Press, 1969), p. xiii.

nation to deny anything like an ontological foundation for ethics of the sort with which we are familiar from the foregoing brief account of natural-law ethics. On the other hand, they are equally determined to try to escape the seeming inevitable consequence of the repudiation of any real objective basis for ethics. That this consequence is serious cannot be disputed; it represents the denial of anything like reason or a rational basis for ethics, with a resultant collapse into what Rosen calls nihilism. But can the consequence be avoided? Can contemporary ethical theorists manage to break out of their dilemma in this way? To answer such questions, let us turn to a brief consideration of the recent history of ethical theory and see for ourselves with what success, or lack of it, the seemingly impossible has been accomplished.

II

ANALYTIC ETHICS:
EARLIER STAGES IN
ITS STRUCTURAL HISTORY

To begin this strange, eventful history, one can perhaps do no better than to start with G. E. Moore. It may not be the most exciting starting point, but at least it has the virtue of being a beginning at the beginning. And yet is it? Doubtless it ought to be made clear at the very outset that the theme of this history is that as soon as one denies any sort of factual status to moral norms or laws, and to values generally, one is somehow brought up sharp by the seeming embarrassing consequence that ethics cannot then be a matter of rational knowledge at all. Given this theme, perhaps one ought to say that Moore is not so much the initiator of that history as merely its forerunner. For Moore, of course, did not deny that goodness was at least in some sense real, or that it was in its odd way a truly objective property [1] of such things as could rightly be called "good." And yet the catch was that this property of goodness could not be equated with or understood in terms of any of the ordinary properties or features or attributes that might actually or conceivably characterize things in the real world. If one did try to understand goodness in terms of any of the

1. Moore himself would doubtless not have characterized "goodness" as an "objective property." Nor is the term itself perhaps an altogether felicitous one. The way we are using it is merely to signify such properties of things in the world as really do pertain to those things as they are in themselves, and not merely as they are relative to us. That this was the import of Moore's insistence in *Principia Ethica* that goodness is a property of things, albeit a non-natural property, is, we believe, scarcely disputable.

known (or even unknown) features of things, this would be to commit the naturalistic fallacy. It would be tantamount to defining goodness in terms of certain of the natural properties of things, and to define goodness in such terms would be simply to reduce it to those terms, thereby rendering goodness itself no more than an ordinary natural property of things in the world.

But this, Moore thinks, is quite impossible, on logical grounds alone. For in the nature of the case any definition must be analytic and such that its opposite is simply inconceivable. Yet no possible definition of goodness in terms, say, of that which is more evolved, or of the pleasurable aspect of things, could ever be such that its opposite would be inconceivable. Suppose, for example, that one were to follow the hedonists and try to define the goodness of anything simply in terms of the pleasure that it gives; would it not be at least meaningful to ask whether the pleasure that something might happen to give—e.g., witnessing the suffering of someone else—is necessarily and as such good and worthwhile? Clearly, though, as Moore sees the matter, the very possibility of asking such a question as to whether pleasure is always and in every instance good implies that it is at least conceivable that goodness is not to be equated with pleasure after all. But if the opposite of a putative definition is at least conceivable, then the putative definition itself immediately ceases to qualify as a definition in the first place. Therefore, Moore considers, this open-question test serves to undercut any and all attempts to define goodness in terms of any of the natural or real properties of things, and so to treat goodness as if it were just an ordinary property like all the rest.[2]

From Moore to Hare:
The Question of the Relevance of Reasons to Ethics

As every one knows, this thesis of Moore's concerning the indefinability of goodness, and concerning that naturalistic fallacy which he thought bound to afflict any proposed definition of goodness, has been subjected to

2. The account just given of Moore's contention that goodness is indefinable is admittedly an interpretive one, adapted to the purposes of our over-all argument. At the same time, we would hope that, as a bit of structural history, it does not misrepresent the thrust of Moore's views in *Principia Ethica*.

no little scrutiny and criticism. But what seems not to have received so much attention,[3] though it has perhaps been no less influential, is a certain consequence of this indefinability of goodness as Moore understood it. This consequence, accepting Moore's thesis of the indefinability of goodness, is that it becomes difficult if not impossible for one ever to give *reasons* for considering something to be good or valuable or worthwhile. In the very logic of the case it would seem that if I say that something is good or worthwhile, and you ask me "Why?" I can answer in all sorts of ways: "Because I like it," or "Because it gives pleasure," or "Because it is personally ennobling," or "Because it contributes to the greater well-being of humankind." Yet ultimately, if I am pressed as to why my liking something, or finding it pleasant, or considering that it makes for the general welfare, should necessarily make it good, I am forced to fall back on something like a definition of goodness, or a declaration as to what goodness by its very nature is.

Thus to use a crude analogy, if I have to give a reason for my judgment that someone is human and not subhuman, and I say it is because he is a language-user, I might then be challenged to explain why being a language-user is necessarily a criterion of being human. To this I reply that language use is no less than a criterion of rationality. But eventually, what I would presumably need to fall back on would be something on the order of a definition of what being human is—e.g., that it is to be a rational animal. Or again, if I have to justify my insisting that a square is a rectangle, might I not proceed by saying that a square is a four-sided figure each of whose angles is a right angle, and that such is what a rectangle is by definition? Very well, then, if to give a reason for something's being x must involve ultimately giving no less than a definition of x,[4] then it

---

3. This statement needs qualification, since in two excellent recent books of readings in contemporary ethics, the editors in their respective prefaces are at pains to point up exactly this development, namely, that Moore's insistence upon the indefinability of goodness leads directly to the denial by the positivists and emotivists of the possibility of good reasons in ethics. See *Theories of Ethics*, ed. Philippa Foot (New York: Oxford University Press, 1967), p. 5; and *Ethics*, ed. J. J. Thomson and G. Dworkin (New York: Harper and Row, 1968), p. 2.

4. We would hope that the scope of the point which is here being made may not be unduly limited as a result of current views as to the meaning of "definition." All that we mean to imply in the logical point that we are here noting is that, by

would appear that, so far as Moore's treatment of goodness is concerned, if good is simply indefinable, there just is no way in which one could ever give any proper reasons in support of one's judgment to the effect that something was good or valuable or worthwhile.

In Moore's own case, it is just at this point that his so-called intuitionism comes into play. When asked why he considers those things to be intrinsically good which he in fact takes to be so, namely, friendships and aesthetic enjoyments, Moore in effect replies that he has no reasons of any kind to support such judgments; instead, he just sees or intuits the goodness of such things.[5]

Somehow, one wonders whether the early readers of *Principia Ethica,* when they reached this high-water mark of Moorean wisdom, would not have been suddenly struck by the fact that the emperor had no clothes. But no, the Lytton Stracheys, the Leonard Woolfs, the John Maynard Keyneses, et al. were just that much more captivated and enthralled by what they saw, or didn't see. In any case, for us today the more charitable course is simply to draw the curtain on Moore at this point, clothes or no clothes. Hurrying on to the next stage in the history, it is not hard to see how it is but a step from Moore's unreasoned goodness to the full-fledged positivism and emotivism of Ayer and Stevenson. True, although Moore did deny to goodness anything like a factual status or status in nature, he certainly did not deny it objective status: goodness was not so much a natural as a non-natural property. To which certain of his more immediate followers simply replied, "Ridiculous!" Rather than let themselves be beguiled into accepting any such mysterious non-natural property of things, they asked, Why not simply recognize that goodness or worth

---

and large, in order to show why a given thing, *a,* necessarily has the property *f,* one needs to have recourse to the kind of thing *a* is, as providing the reason for *a*'s being *f.* If, then, by "definition" one means no more than a statement as to what a thing is or the kind of thing it is, without any necessary implication that such definitions cannot be other than "analytic," all well and good. For this broader and now somewhat unorthodox view of definition, see our earlier book, *Two Logics* (Evanston: Northwestern University Press, 1969), esp. chap. 3.

5. See *Principia Ethica* (Cambridge: At the University Press, 1929), esp. chaps. 4 and 5.

just isn't a property of things at all? Why not consider that good is really not even a properly descriptive term in the first place? Rather it is a term used to express our approval of something, as well as our recommendation or command that others approve it as well.

Indeed, it perhaps would not be amiss to recall once more that youthful exhibition of nose-thumbing to which the young A. J. Ayer treated the then somewhat staid and stuffy philosophical world:

> The presence of an ethical symbol in a proposition adds nothing to its factual content. Thus if I say to someone, "You acted wrongly in stealing that money," I am not stating anything more than if I had simply said, "You stole that money." In adding that this action is wrong I am not making any further statement about it. I am simply evincing my moral disapproval of it. It is as if I had said, "You stole that money," in a peculiar tone of horror, or written it with the addition of some special exclamation marks. The tone, or the exclamation marks, adds nothing to the literal meaning of the sentence. It merely serves to show that the expression of it is attended by certain feelings in the speaker.
>
> If now I generalize my previous statement and say, "Stealing money is wrong," I produce a sentence which has no factual meaning—that is, expresses no proposition which can be either true or false. It is as if I had written "Stealing money!!"—where the shape and thickness of the exclamation marks show, by a suitable convention, that a special sort of moral disapproval is the feeling which is being expressed.[6]

No sooner, though, does one begin to talk in this vein than one would seem, whether inadvertently or by design, to have undercut the very possibility of morals or ethics having any kind of a reasoned or evidential basis at all. For let one but distinguish, as Ayer insists must be done, between the purely factual element in a moral judgment—e.g., the fact that "you stole that money"—and the attitude of moral disapproval or the feeling of horror which is evinced by a particular moral judgment, and what is the result? The result clearly is that there would no longer seem to be any

6. A. J. Ayer, *Language, Truth and Logic,* 2d ed. (London: Victor Gollancz, 1946), p. 107.

sort of rational basis or ground for that moral disapproval or feeling of horror which the judgment is taken to evince.

To point the contrast rather crudely, not to say naively, suppose that distinctions between good and bad, or right and wrong, did have a certain objective, ontological status in the facts themselves. Then it would become readily understandable how one has but to acknowledge that a given action or mode of behavior is really right or really wrong, and at once a thoroughly rational ground is provided for such attitudes of approval or disapproval as one's moral judgments might express. Deny, on the other hand, that moral distinctions or value distinctions have any objective status in the facts, and it then becomes at least problematic whether one's pro- or con-attitudes have any rational justification at all. Indeed, the way in which this issue obtrudes itself into the context of emotivism, particularly when this latter sort of ethical theory is seen against its Moorean background, is something like this: Moore, in effect, had found himself unable in principle to specify any reasons why the non-natural property of goodness should supervene upon the various natural properties which in a given case might be held to be good; in turn the emotivists, by denying to goodness any objective status of any kind, neither could nor cared to explain how or why our feelings of approval or disapproval toward utterly valueless and morally neutral facts should have any rational basis or justification.

For that matter, C. L. Stevenson, who elaborated emotivist theory to a point of utmost refinement, would appear to have come right out and admitted that while of course there might be various causes for the moral judgments and value judgments that we make, there could not properly be any reasons for such judgments.

> The reasons which support or attack an ethical judgment have previously been mentioned. Subject to some exceptions that will be noted as we proceed, they are related to the judgment psychologically rather than logically. They do not strictly imply the judgment in the way that axioms imply theorems; nor are they related to the judgment inductively, as statements describing observations are related to scientific laws. Rather they support the judgment in the way that reasons support imperatives. They serve to intensify and render more permanent the influence upon

attitudes which emotive meaning can often do no more than begin. This is possible whenever attitudes are functions of belief.[7]

To go into rather more detail on just how this tendency to displace reasons in favor of causes works out in Stevenson's ethics, it will be remembered that Stevenson was certainly more clear, if not actually more unequivocal, than Ayer in recognizing that there can be genuine disagreement in matters of ethics. But the disagreement may be of two kinds, or, perhaps better, may involve two different moments, "disagreements in belief" (or disagreement as to the facts) and "disagreement in attitude." For example, Stevenson in his so-called working model of an analysis of "This is good" suggests that what is involved is really a statement to the effect, "I approve of this; do so as well." Accordingly, in disagreeing with such a judgment and in insisting "This is not good," one might either take issue with what the facts are that are being referred to by "this"; or one might agree as to the facts and take issue with the approval and the imperative that are expressed.

Suppose, though, the question is raised as to just what the connection is between what might be called the factual pole and the attitudinal or imperatival pole of an ethical judgment. Or to put the same question in terms of the possibility of ethical agreement and disagreement, does agreement or disagreement as to the facts of the case have any bearing on the matter of agreement or disagreement in attitude? Stevenson, as is well known, would answer this question in the affirmative. Yet the significance of his affirmative answer is that such bearing as the one may have on the other can only be causal and not properly rational at all. As he says, "A

---

7. C. L. Stevenson, *Ethics and Language* (New Haven: Yale University Press, 1944), p. 113. It is perhaps ironical that in the very quotation which we cite in order to show how Stevenson denies the possibility of reasons in ethics, he begins by talking about "reasons" for an ethical judgment. However, it should be clear from the context that what Stevenson here calls "reasons" are the very things which later linguistic philosophers would have been careful to term "causes." While all of this probably calls for a full-scale discussion of the difference (and the relation) between reasons and causes, it would lead us too far afield. The more patent differences between these two notions should appear simply from the contexts of their use, which should suffice for the limited purposes of the present discussion.

reasoned agreement . . . is theoretically possible only to the extent that agreement in belief will *cause* people to agree in attitude." [8]

W. D. Hudson, who quotes this passage in his book *Modern Moral Philosophy,* proceeds to comment on it quite sternly, not to say emotively:

> It will be seen at once that this is indeed "a substitute for proof." There is the world of difference between providing one's hearer with *reasons* for adopting an attitude (or anything else) and saying things that will cause him to do so. This is the feature which characterizes, and vitiates, Stevenson's whole ethical theory. Subtle and, in many ways, illuminating as that theory is, in the last analysis it fails because it reduces logical to psychological considerations.[9]

Such words of rebuke from Hudson are indicative of how, in the history of analytic ethics, such ethical emotivism and non-cognitivism as Ayer's and Stevenson's soon occasioned serious misgivings. The source of these misgivings might be summed up in the very point which was enunciated briefly in the conclusion of the last chapter: if ethical judgments are in principle incapable of ever being reasoned judgments, then either there is no such thing as ethics, or ethics is itself no better than a fraud. Accordingly, the subsequent history of analytic ethics, after the early move from Moore to emotivism, would seem to be largely a history of attempts to rehabilitate the possibility of adducing something like genuine rational bases and grounds for our moral judgments and value judgments generally, and yet without our being thereby committed to a recognition of anything like a factual status for values, to say nothing of a "natural" status for moral laws and norms.

Can such a thing be done, though? That is the issue we should like to raise with respect to various of the more recent developments in analytic ethics. To do so, however, we must examine the developments themselves, which brings us to that most awesome of contemporary ethical theorists of the analytic school, R. M. Hare.

8. *Ibid.,* p. 31.
9. W. D. Hudson, *Modern Moral Philosophy* (Garden City, N. Y.: Doubleday, Anchor Books, 1970), pp. 120–21.

Hare to the Rescue:
"Good Reasons" in Ethics Must Be Saved!

There is no question that Hare conceived it to be at least partly his enterprise in *The Language of Morals* to rehabilitate the reasoned character of ethical judgments, certainly against the emotivists and presumably against Moore as well. But what is especially noteworthy and, from the standpoint of the thesis which we are trying to defend in this book, particularly disturbing is Hare's conviction that he can secure good reasons in support of ethical judgments without having to fall back on the supposedly antediluvian and hence ante-Moorean view that goodness and value have no less than an objective status right in the world of fact. One could very properly describe *The Language of Morals* as a brilliant effort to shatter once and for all any alleged tie-up between reasons in ethics and the supposition that ethical distinctions and properties are themselves genuine matters of fact.[10]

To this end, Hare both accepts Moore's naturalistic fallacy argument and seeks to sharpen it and extend its scope. Not only is it the case that values cannot be equated with facts, but value words have a very distinct linguistic role or function of their own to perform in judgments, namely, that of commending or prescribing things, as over against describing them. Moreover, when one does attempt to equate, say, the goodness or excellence of a thing with various of its objective properties, then what immediately drops out of the picture is that very act of commending or approving which it was quite patently the function of the value word to perform. It is difficult to show this decisively in terms of examples, simply because so many terms that are primarily descriptive come to take on evaluative overtones in certain contexts (and, conversely, even evaluative

10. For the ensuing analysis and criticism of Hare's position, as well as the positions of Foot and Searle in the next chapter, I am much indebted to three recent doctoral dissertations, all unpublished, that have recently been submitted at Northwestern—those of Ronald Duska, Sheldon Cohen, and Michael Robins. While I am eager to acknowledge my debt to all three, I should not want it thought that any of them is to be associated with any of the conclusions arrived at in this book.

terms often acquire a descriptive force in a given context). Still the point can be made abstractly if one will but recognize that to describe something is not just to commend it, and, vice versa, to commend it is indeed to do something different from merely describing it. Hence to try simply to reduce the one to the other is to do linguistic violence to both at once.[11]

Nevertheless, as we have already noted, Hare's insistence upon the prescriptive rather than the descriptive force of value words is coupled with an equal insistence upon what he takes to be a no less inescapable fact of language use, namely, that the very use of prescriptive or evaluative terms immediately implies the logical relevance of reasons in support of such prescriptions and evaluations. Thus to resort to a somewhat elementary example, just consider the difference between the following collocutions or locution patterns:

1. I say: "I like spinach."
   You ask: "Why?"
   I answer: "I don't know why; I just like it, that's all."

2. I say: "I ought to eat spinach," or "Spinach is good for me."
   You ask: "Why?"
   I answer: "Because it is nutritious," or "Because of its high vitamin content."

Such contrasting examples may serve to bring out more clearly the difference between the relevance of *reasons* for ethical judgments, as over against the relevance of *causes* of such judgments. Thus mere likes and dislikes certainly do have causes, psychological, physiological, sociological, or what not; but they do not necessarily have reasons. In contrast, no sooner is an actual value judgment made, to say nothing of a moral judgment, than reasons for the judgment, as over against mere causes, immediately become relevant.

Now it is just such a point as this last that Hare constantly reiterates. Indeed, Hudson comments on Hare's view to this effect:

---

11. For Hare's own most telling arguments in support of this, see *The Language of Morals* (Oxford: Clarendon Press, 1952), esp. pt. 2, chap. 5.

Value-words, i.e. words such as "good," "right," and "ought," have, according to Hare, a "supervenient character." He arrived at this conclusion by reflecting upon certain features of their ordinary use. It is, for instance, *always* logically legitimate to ask for a reason when value judgments have been delivered. Take these examples: "This is a good book," "This is the right road," "You ought to pay your tailor's bill." In every case it would be in order for the person so addressed to ask "Why?" And the answer to the question typically would be some naturalistic description of the thing concerned, e.g., "The characters in this book are very funny," "This road will take us to our destination," "Your tailor made you a suit on the understanding that you would pay for it." The justification, or ground, of goodness, or rightness, or oughtness respectively lies in certain non-evaluative characteristics of the thing or action to be judged.[12]

So be it! Indeed, let us readily concede for the moment that by such appeal to nothing more nor less than linguistic use, Hare has made his case both for the fact (1) that value words are used always in the first instance prescriptively, and hence can never be used so as to describe real values existing in the world, and (2) that whenever value words are used, it is necessarily implied that there are certain factual or naturalistic or non-evaluative considerations that are relevant as reasons in support of such evaluations. Does this not, then, settle the matter?

Hardly, for we still need to have explained just what the nature is of that connection between our prescriptions or evaluations and those purely factual or non-evaluative considerations that are supposed to be adduced in justification of them. After all, it was a by no means dissimilar issue which, as we saw earlier, the emotivists had to face up to and rather signally failed to resolve. Thus with reference to Ayer's example, the question was: suppose that someone did in fact steal money, why and on what grounds might this be supposed to provide anyone with a reason for moral disapproval of such action? To such a question the emotivists in effect had no answer; or rather their answer was that while there might be causes for such a reaction of disapproval, there were no reasons for it.

But now Hare comes along and insists that of course there are reasons for such a thing. In any moral judgment or value judgment our moral or

12. Hudson, *Modern Moral Philosophy*, p. 164.

29

value words are used prescriptively—i.e., they are used in a way that is not descriptive but "action-guiding." Still more specifically, Hare says, they are used to commend. Very well, then, if our commendations are thus regarded as somehow supervening upon such beliefs as we may have about the facts of the case, just why and how are such facts able to function as reasons for our commendations? Are the facts somehow commendable in themselves? Hare could never say this, for it would be tantamount not only to committing the naturalistic fallacy but also to turning prescriptions and evaluations into descriptions. How otherwise, though, is Hare to account for the reasoned character of our prescriptions and evaluations?

That there is indeed a logical connection between our evaluations and the factual considerations that we cite as being reasons for them Hare makes abundantly clear.[13] His example, by way of illustration, is that of two pictures which are exactly alike in all respects. In such a case, Hare says, we could not—i.e., logically or properly—call the one picture "good" and refuse to acknowledge the other to be good also.[14] Indeed, this example might be taken to point up as sharply as possible the difference between Hare's position and that of the emotivists. For Stevenson, in considering the question of whether agreement in belief might have any bearing on agreement in attitude, unhesitatingly answered in the affirmative: There is often, indeed, a connection between agreement or disagreement in belief and in attitude. But, then, Stevenson hastens to add, the connection "is always factual, never logical."[15]

For Hare, then, it is clearly a logical and not a mere factual connection that holds between a set of facts and such evaluations as may supervene upon them. Still, just what is the nature of this logical connection?

It is not a connection of logical entailment, Hare declares. That is to say, we may not suppose that there is a set of characteristics which might be said to entail a thing's being good, much as there would indeed be a set of characteristics which could certainly be said to entail the picture's being rectangular, supposing that it were rectangular.[16] Any such entail-

---

13. See the decisive statement to this effect in *Language of Morals,* p. 111.
14. *Ibid.,* pp. 80–81.
15. Hudson, *Modern Moral Philosophy,* p. 118.
16. See Hare, *Language of Morals,* pp. 81–82.

ment relationship between the natural properties of an object and its goodness would be tantamount to the sort of thing which we described earlier
as being an effort to understand the reasons for a thing's being good in
terms of what "good" means or the definition of goodness. And this, Hare
contends, would never do, because it would be simply a case of committing
the naturalistic fallacy.

Very well, then, if in Hare's eyes the relation between the "good-making
properties" of a thing and its goodness is not and cannot be a relation of
entailment, just what sort of a logical relation or connection is it? So far
as we have been able to understand Hare's answer to this question in *The
Language of Morals,* it turns on the logical distinction (and also the logical connection) between the meaning of a term—in this case the term
"good"—and the criteria of its application.[17] Nor can one possibly deny
the legitimacy of the point which Hare is here making, at least so far
as it goes. For certainly we do pronounce to be "good" things as diverse
and heterogeneous as cricket bats, chronometers, strawberries, motor cars,
and men. Moreover, the meaning of "good" could scarcely be said to vary
from instance to instance in such cases;[18] and yet quite obviously the
criteria of goodness or excellence in motor cars are very different from
what they are for strawberries, and those for strawberries very different
from those for chronometers, and those for chronometers different from
those for men, and so on.

In other words, the differences in the criteria for the application of the
word "good" in various contexts clearly show that the relation between
the natural properties of a thing and its supervenient goodness or excellence cannot be an entailment relation or a relation based on the definition
of goodness. Yet there is surely some relation—and a logical relation at
that—between the natural properties of an object and the fact that we
call it "good," which is evidenced by the fact that these same criteria for
the application of the word "good" in different contexts may also be re-

17. *Ibid.,* esp. chap. 6.

18. Subsequently, when we come to a fuller discussion of our own proposals for
an ontology of morals, we shall argue that "goodness" is not a univocal term at all,
but rather an analogous one. However, we may agree with Hare for the present
that although the meaning of "good" remains the same, the criteria of its application vary according to the sort of thing that is being pronounced good.

garded as the reasons for our calling such different things "good." Thus, "Why do you say that the car is a good car?" "Because of its speed, its maneuverability, its economy to operate, etc." Or, "Why is that strawberry a good one?" "Because it is large, red, juicy, ripe, etc."

With this, then, has not Hare made his case? If he has not specified exactly, he has at least sought to illustrate what sort of a logical relation or connection may be presumed to hold between the natural properties of a given object and the evaluation that we place upon it. Besides, he would seem to have done this without conceding to values or to moral distinctions any sort of ontological status or status in fact or in the nature of things. What more could one ask?

Are Hare's "Good Reasons"
More Like Non-Reasons?

Perhaps, though, there is just one thing more: Has Hare ever explained just what there is about such criteria or reasons for the application of the word "good" that fits them to be, or renders them, criteria or reasons? And if our question at first seems gratuitous and farfetched, it is prompted by Hare's own account of that very illocutionary force which the use of value words and moral terms is supposed to have. For such words are used not descriptively, but rather prescriptively and as action-guiding. Moreover, Hare sums up the peculiar prescriptive or action-guiding character of a word such as "good" by saying that it is used to commend. What is more, such commendation is never without reasons. All of this, indeed, is evidenced simply by the facts of linguistic use.

Still, when I undertake to commend something or to evince a pro-attitude toward it, just what is there about the facts of the case that would lead me to commend it rather than not, or to feel a pro-attitude toward it rather than a con-attitude? Suppose, for example, that a particular human being is wise, just, courageous, willing to act, inflexible in his resolutions, etc. And suppose these qualities of the man are no more than mere "natural properties" [19] which he simply has as a matter of fact. Just

19. Needless to say, the virtues just enumerated can hardly be reckoned as but so many neutral natural properties. Words like "wise" or "courageous" have a

why is it that I should commend the person for such qualities rather than not? Or why should I commend him for these qualities rather than for an entirely different set of qualities, say?

Now such questions are surely pertinent, inasmuch as, on Hare's analysis, "good" is a prescriptive rather than a descriptive term, and thus to call a man "good" who has qualities or virtues such as those just enumerated is not to say that such qualities have a worth or value in themselves and in fact, and apart from my approval or commendation of them. That would be to pervert the use of "good" from being a prescriptive to being a descriptive term, and would commit the naturalistic fallacy into the bargain. Granted. But that serves to make our questions all the more telling. For if there is nothing in the facts of the case, or nothing in the natural properties of the object, that could in any proper sense be considered really and in fact commendable, then why should we commend it? Or why should the reasons that we give for commending what we do be reasons at all, rather than non-reasons?

Perhaps we might point up the issue even more sharply by availing ourselves of a somewhat old-fashioned formula that was not uncommon in the eighteenth century as a sort of touchstone for ethics. The formula can be put in the form of a question: Are things desired because they are good, or good because they are desired? We would not be forcing either the formula or its relevance to the present-day ethical situation if, instead of "desired," we were to substitute the word "commended." Do we, in other words, commend things because they are good; or rather are they good merely because and insofar as we commend them? Now surely Hare, were he to be confronted with alternatives such as these, would have to opt for the latter, rather than the former. For to suppose that things were commended because they were in fact and in themselves good would in Hare's eyes be, if not to commit the naturalistic fallacy, to confound the prescriptive use of "good" with description. Accordingly,

---

prescriptive or evaluative force built right into them that is hardly separable from their descriptive meaning. However, it is difficult to find purely neutral words that would be suitable for illustration; and so we are using words that are admittedly value-laden, but asking that they be considered in terms of their descriptive force alone.

for him things may be said to be "good" only because we commend them —in fact, to call them "good" simply is to commend them.

Note, though, what the implications of such a response would be in regard to the various sets of criteria that are to serve for the application of the word "good." For the criteria will have no sort of independent status, such as might enable them to determine or justify our commendation. Rather it is simply in virtue of a decision on our part to commend something of such and such a kind that the properties of the thing thus commended may then be reckoned as criteria for the application to it of the word "good."

Indeed, let us spell out this particular point a bit crudely, not only with respect to the so-called criteria of goodness but also with respect to the so-called reasons that one may have for calling a thing "good." Thus suppose that, following Hare, I do commend a car for its speed, maneuverability, etc.[20] Just why do I commend it for having these traits rather than others? What is there about speed, maneuverability, or what not—considered simply as objective properties of the thing or object—that renders a car possessed of these properties commendable, whereas one possessed of other properties would not be so?

Somehow, we think that Hare would have to reply that there is nothing about these traits as such that makes them good or commendable in themselves. But if there is nothing about the *traits* that makes a car possessed of them commendable, then it cannot be by reason of such properties that I commend it. Rather, it must be because I commend the thing in the first place that its properties take on such a semblance of value and commendability. Clearly, though, if the supposed reasons for my commendation are reasons only *as a result* of my commendation, then they can scarcely be proper reasons *for* my commendation. Thus it would indeed seem that the logic of ethical judgments—at least as Hare construes it—would have the effect of turning good reasons into a species of non-reasons.

20. The next few paragraphs reproduce with very little alteration an argument that was worked out in an earlier article of ours entitled "Good Reasons and Prescriptivism in Ethics," *Ethics*, LXXX, no. 2 (January, 1970), esp. 106–7.

For an Ontology of Morals
A Critique of Contemporary Ethical Theory

by Henry B. Veatch

Professor Veatch's initial thesis is that contemporary ethical theories, those of the analysts and of the existentialists alike, are unable to provide us with any recourse in ethical theory other than ethical nihilism. As a second thesis, he suggests that contemporary ethical theorists might be able to avoid this devastating criticism by using a particular Kantian philosophical device, the transcendental turn. Although it has been standard practice among both analysts and existentialists to use this device in other areas of their philosophies, it has never been used in the area of ethics proper. Accordingly, the author applies the transcendental turn in both analytic and existentialist ethics. The result, however, is shown ultimately to be of no help.

This failure is then used as a means of introducing the major and final thesis of the book, which is that ethics is presently in serious need of an ontology of morals or ethics, rather than an analytic "language of morals" or a phenomenology of morals. This is followed by an analysis of just what an ontological or factual status of moral and ethical distinctions must involve, as well as by a defense of this more traditional type of ethical theory as over against its more fashionable modern rivals, utilitarianism and Kantianism.

Henry B. Veatch is John Evans Professor of Philosophy at Northwestern University. He is the author of *Intentional Logic; Rational Man;* and (with Francis Parker) *Logic as a Human Instrument.* His most recent book, *Two Logics: The Conflict between Classical and Neo-Analytic Philosophy,* is published by Northwestern University Press.

$6.50

Pursuing this same line of consideration still further, we believe that so-called criteria in Hare's sense are not even criteria. Instead, the logic of one of Hare's typical evaluative or prescriptive situations would appear to be quite radically different from what Hare would at times seem inclined to represent it as being. Supposing now, in view of our foregoing considerations, that commendation is a thing for which there are and can be no good reasons; it would seem then that such commendation would have to be comparatively specific. Again employing Hare's example of the car, it is not cars as such that we commend, but only those which are fast, maneuverable, and economical to operate. In other words, what we commend in such a case are not cars in general, but only cars of type *X,* shall we say.

No sooner do we explicate an evaluative or prescriptive situation in this way than one can promptly see that the properties of speed, maneuverability, economy, etc., are not criteria for the application of the word "good"; instead, they are no more than criteria for the application of the term "motor car of type *X.*" In other words, it is only because we have already decided to call motor cars of type *X* "good" that the particular properties in terms of which we happen to have defined cars of that type become relevant to the situation at all. But they are scarcely relevant as criteria for the application of the word "good," at least not in the sense of providing reasons for calling cars of that type "good" or for commending them. Rather, it is only because cars having those properties have been called "good" in the first place that such properties might be said to have any connection with goodness at all.

Has Hare succeeded, after all, in restoring "good reasons" to ethics, following upon the emotivists' determined effort to extrude them? Somehow, we cannot help feeling that Hare has done little more than to make the word "reasons," but hardly the thing itself, respectable in ethics once again. For that matter, there are at least some among the more recent moral philosophers in England who have shown what would almost amount to a decided irritation with respect to Hare on this score, as if he had somehow played fast and loose with them in regard to the whole business of good reasons in ethics. It is thus that Hudson represents the views of those disillusioned with Hare:

35

The telling point which [these critics] have to make is that both emotivism and prescriptivism do not simply consider it possible on moral issues for us to make up our mind *on* the evidence, but no less possible for us to make up our own minds what shall count as evidence. To quote Warnock . . ."I do not, it seems, decide that flogging is wrong because I *am* against cruelty; rather, I decide that flogging is wrong because I *decide to be* against cruelty. And what, if I did make that decision, would be my ground for making it? That I am opposed to the deliberate infliction of pain? No—rather that I *decide to be* opposed to it. And so on." There are people, he goes on, who make up not only their own minds, but also their own evidence; but such people are a menace, not a model, not exemplars of, but abstainers from, reasoning.[21]

After this brief exposé of Hare, so far as his defense of good reasons in ethics is concerned, we end this chapter on something of an "I-told-you-so" note. Could it be that the source of Hare's difficulties on this issue is traceable directly to the fact that he seeks to justify our prescriptions, evaluations, and commendations at the same time that he stoutly refuses to admit of anything of worth or value or excellence in the facts that could ever serve as a rational basis for our purportedly reasoned prescriptions, evaluations, and commendations? But one simply cannot have one's cake and eat it too. Nor perhaps can one ever make do with a mere language of morals, it being rather an ontology of morals that is the prime requisite. Still, we ought not to put this forward as something that can already be seen, when it still for the most part remains to be seen.

21. Hudson, *Modern Moral Philosophy,* p. 207.

III

ANALYTIC ETHICS:
LATER STAGES IN
ITS STRUCTURAL HISTORY

Quite patently in the preceding chapters our attempted structural history of analytic ethics, like "vaulting ambition," must have seemed to "o'erleap itself and fall on the other." It might be said that rather than let the inadequacies of Hare's account of good reasons in ethics appear directly and exclusively within the context of linguistic analysis, we tended to go outside that context altogether, and from the totally alien context of a natural-law ethics to argue that no mere appeal to linguistic use could ever suffice to justify the effort to find good reasons in support of our moral and value judgments. Hence the ax that we had to grind was presumably all too much in evidence: no mere linguistic warrant but only an ontological warrant could ever be adequate as a means of legitimating our inveterate human tendency to try to find reasons in support of our ethical judgments. Surely, this is getting ahead of ourselves!

The Reaction against Hare

But why fall back into the dark, discredited catacombs of so-called natural law? Would not the resources of linguistic analysis itself appear sufficient to expose the insufficiencies of Hare's account of good reasons? Indeed, it is now almost twenty years since *The Language of Morals* first appeared. And since that time, although Hare has been made White's

Professor of Moral Philosophy in the University of Oxford, it would seem that many of the Oxford philosophers themselves, and others of their ilk, have become increasingly dissatisfied with his teaching—at least on the score of good reasons in ethics. Thus Philippa Foot, to cite but one example, in a much-discussed paper, "Moral Beliefs," not only declares her manifest dissatisfaction with Hare's position but has even had the temerity to open her paper by suggesting that perhaps the old issue of ethical naturalism, which presumably G. E. Moore had laid to a rest from which there could be no conceivable resurrection, should perhaps be revived after all.[1]

Specifically, the fault which she finds with Hare is that, in acceding so uncritically to the long-current repudiation of naturalism, he had inadvertently got himself into a position where just anything at all might conceivably be reckoned as a "good reason" for an evaluation, moral or otherwise. But this, Mrs. Foot thinks, is simply untenable. How, she asks, could the fact that a man is given to clasping and unclasping his hands, or that he never turns NNE after turning SSW, ever be a good reason for considering him to be a good man?[2] Such a thing is nothing less than preposterous.

Indeed, to consider some examples that are outside the proper domain of ethical evaluations but that are still analogous, Mrs. Foot asks us to consider such things as fear and pride. Is it not obvious that there are "limits to the things a man can be proud of, about which he can feel pride?"[3] Save only in very special circumstances, could one ever suppose that a person could be proud of the sea or take pride in the sky? Or how about a man's being proud of his having laid one hand on the other three times in an hour? Presumably, though, on Hare's view, the meaning

---

1. "Moral Beliefs" originally appeared in *Proceedings of the Aristotelian Society,* Vol. 59 (1958–59), pp. 83–104. Since then this very significant article has been anthologized both in Mrs. Foot's own book of readings, *Theories of Ethics* (New York: Oxford University Press, 1967), pp. 83–100, and in J. J. Thomson and G. Dworkin's *Ethics* (New York: Harper and Row, 1968), pp. 239–60. Unless otherwise specified our references will be to the article as reprinted in the former of these two volumes.

2. Foot, "Moral Beliefs," p. 84.

3. *Ibid.,* p. 85.

of the term "proud of" being one thing and the criteria of its application another, we need only *decide* in a given case—say, that of natural expanses like the sky and the sea, or that of human beings and their achievements —that the criteria of the term's application are to be such and such, and then things like the sky or the sea, or certain actions of our own like clasping our hands together, could perfectly well qualify as objects of pride. Yet isn't this rather farfetched? Mrs. Foot asks.

Likewise, in regard to fear, Mrs. Foot brings forward a number of telling examples to show that fear is something which may properly be experienced only in the face of what is really dangerous. And if one tries to make out that "dangerous" is not a property-word at all, and that, so far from designating anything in the object, it is only a "practical or action-guiding term, used for warning," then Mrs. Foot counters by pointing out that unless there were something in the object to warrant our thinking it dangerous and thus as something about which people should be warned, then the warning no less than the belief in the danger would be simply misplaced.[4]

In fact, according to Mrs. Foot, the weakness in Hare's view of reasons in ethics is that, having made so sharp a separation between what is there in the facts and our evaluation of the facts, Hare is unable to make it clear why certain facts any more than others should serve as reasons for evaluations and commendations.[5] In consequence, as Mrs. Foot sees it, Hare makes two quite indefensible assumptions about evaluations and pro-attitudes:

Assumption (1) is that some individual may, without logical error, base his belief about matters of value entirely on premises which no one else would recognize as giving any evidence at all. Assumption (2) is that,

---

4. *Ibid.,* p. 87.

5. In fairness, it should be recognized that Hare does insist upon at least consistency in such matters. As the example of the two pictures which was cited in the foregoing chapter shows, if a certain property or set of properties in an object is ever once a reason for our calling such an object good, then it is always and equally a reason for calling any other object good that has the same property or properties. However, what is not clear in Hare is why any property or set of properties should ever be held to constitute a reason for calling the thing good in the first place.

given the kind of statement which other people regard as evidence for an evaluative conclusion, he may refuse to draw the conclusion because *this* does not count as evidence for *him*.[6]

Oddly enough, though, for all of her skill in faulting Hare's account of good reasons in ethics, it would seem that Mrs. Foot's own account thereof does not come through as clearly and unambiguously as one might wish. For just what is at the root of her criticism of Hare? Is it that Hare fails to recognize that when in the light of *linguistic* considerations it becomes apparent that we properly may and do appeal to the facts of the case in support of our evaluations of those facts, then this can only be because *ontologically,* and not just linguistically, values do have a real or objective basis in the facts? If, indeed, this were the line of criticism that Mrs. Foot wished to take, then it would be hard to distinguish her criticism of Hare from such criticism as might be mounted by defenders of traditional natural-law ethics. Still, it is entirely possible, and not at all clear from the texts, that the redoubtable Mrs. Foot would rather be dead than be found consorting with any such questionable philosophical company as natural-law moralists.

It is true that when Mrs. Foot comes to discuss the use of a predicate like "dangerous," she seems to be saying that we cannot suppose that to call something "dangerous" could be no more than an idiosyncratic warning, or that people could properly call even the oddest things dangerous. In addition, she seems to imply that to be dangerous is no less a real property of certain objects, and that it is a property that can attach only to "a particular kind of serious evil such as injury or death."[7] Still, unequivocal as this might seem to the analytically uninitiated, it is at least conceivable that such pronouncements by Mrs. Foot are to be interpreted as having only a linguistic and not at all an ontological import. That is to say, *talk* about being dangerous might well be inescapably bound up with *talk* about real injuries or even death. But this might be

---

6. Foot, "Moral Beliefs," p. 84.
7. *Ibid.,* p. 87.

construed as being no more than a matter of talk, i.e., of linguistic rules, and not a matter of ontological commitment at all.[8]

Professor Searle:

A New Departure in Analytic Ethics?

Enough, though, with respect to Mrs. Foot. Let us pass on quickly to John R. Searle. It could just be that at the very point where Foot was found to be ambiguous and indecisive, Searle may turn out to be unequivocal and unmistakable. Nor is there any denying the fact that when the young Searle's earlier article on "How to Derive 'Ought' from 'Is' " burst on the unprepared and decorous readers of the *Philosophical Review*,[9] this young analyst did indeed manage to "flutter the proud Salopians like an eagle in a dove cot." At first glance, one might even wonder whether Searle—albeit perhaps somewhat naively and even unwittingly—were not bent on simply brushing away all of the remaining obstacles so as to lead the sheeplike analysts right back into the long-abandoned camp of the natural-law philosophers.

Consider once again just what the issue is. As we have seen, the hallmark of a natural-law ethics is that norms and values are held to be based or grounded in nature, and that in virtue of norms thus having a natural status, as over against being merely man-made, it is possible to claim a rational basis for ethics. In contrast, a linguistic analyst like Hare,

8. That this is indeed Mrs. Foot's view can be gathered from certain remarks made in another of her articles entitled "Moral Arguments" (reprinted in Thomson and Dworkin, *Ethics,* see p. 17). Here Mrs. Foot makes it clear that she considers it to be no more than a matter of linguistic rules (and hence not of ontological commitment), which upon occasion "forbid the assertion of factual propositions in conjunction with the denial of moral propositions." For a most illuminating discussion of Mrs. Foot's position, see chap. 6 of the dissertation of Ronald Duska already referred to above (Chapter II, n. 10).

9. LXXIII (1964), 43–58. This article has also been anthologized in Foot, *Theories of Ethics,* pp. 101–14. In Searle's subsequent book, *Speech Acts* (Cambridge: At the University Press, 1969), the argument of his earlier article is substantially reproduced in chap. 8.

while vigorously insisting that moral judgments and value judgments are capable of being rationally grounded, nevertheless steadfastly refuses to concede any ontological or factual status in nature to such things as norms and values. And yet is such a position as Hare's really tenable? Does it come down to anything more than a sort of linguistic sleight of hand, whereby he no sooner makes an ontological bestowal with his right hand than he takes it back linguistically with his left? That is the question.

Witness now Searle. At first he does come on rather dashingly, and, for an analytic philosopher, manages to say things that sound almost like a kind of *lèse-majesté* with respect to analysis itself. For instance, going counter to the entire tradition of analytic ethics from Moore on, he jauntily talks about "the naturalistic fallacy fallacy." After all, the naturalistic fallacy, remember, was precisely Moore's ploy to show that value predicates simply cannot be equated with any of the real or natural features of the world. To this Searle simply responds by bringing forward various examples that would seem to show quite unequivocally that so-called evaluative notions and predicates can be, and often are, defined in terms of straightforward descriptive properties.[10]

One such example is taken from the British Ministry of Agriculture and Fisheries, where the term "Extra Fancy Grade" is employed for grading apples. Quite patently this is a term of evaluation. Yet note that if one asks what "Extra Fancy Grade" means in this connection, it means apples having properties (if you will, "natural properties") *A, B,* and *C,* these latter being purely descriptive. In other words, the definition of the evaluative term for grading apples is unmistakably and unreservedly in terms of certain natural (or descriptive) properties of apples.[11]

An even more striking example of Searle's seeming willingness to return to what might be called a naturalistic position in ethics—in the sense of a position in which norms and values are held to have a status right in the very nature of things—is his celebrated exhibition of how an "ought" can be derived from an "is." Even the mere project of such a derivation would appear to constitute a direct challenge to that entire modern

10. Searle, *Speech Acts,* pp. 132 ff.
11. *Ibid.,* pp. 135–36.

tradition in ethics which demands of its partisans an answering faithful-
ness to the principles of the ultimate separation of values from facts and
of ethics from nature. Along with G. E. Moore's naturalistic fallacy,
Hume's warning against trying to derive an "ought" from an "is" was
one of the very foundation stones of analytic ethics. Or, coming at the
matter from the opposite side, just as any denial that the naturalistic
fallacy is a fallacy would seem to hold out the promise that ethical knowledge might once again be reintegrated into an over-all natural knowledge,
so also any suggestion that an "ought" might be derived from an "is"
would appear at once to revive the possibility that there are such things as
natural laws and natural norms after all. Since a law is nothing but a
prescribing or prohibiting of certain actions, it would surely seem to
follow that if a law were held to be natural, such a prescribing or prohibiting must itself be something natural, something that is justified
literally by the nature of the case.

Very well, then, let us come directly to Searle's project of deriving
"ought" from "is." Surely, everyone is by now familiar with how Searle
sought to bring off such a derivation by an exhibit of five statements,
of which each succeeding one might readily be seen, or at least be
shown, to follow from the one immediately preceding:

1. Jones uttered the words "I hereby promise to pay you, Smith, five
   dollars."
2. Jones promised to pay Smith five dollars.
3. Jones placed himself under (undertook) an obligation to pay
   Smith five dollars.
4. Jones is under an obligation to pay Smith five dollars.
5. Jones ought to pay Smith five dollars.[12]

And there it is! By such a simple exhibit of five propositions Searle
thinks that he has shown how the mere fact of making a promise involves
or carries with it a moral obligation to carry out that promise. Q.E.D.!

Is it really a case of Q.E.D., though? It is not surprising that the validity

---

12. This supposed derivation of an "ought" from an "is" appears both in Searle's
article, "How to Derive 'Ought' from 'Is,'" p. 102, and in *Speech Acts*, p. 177.

of Searle's demonstration should have been vigorously debated in the literature.[13] However, for purposes of the sort of structural history that we are here seeking to sketch out, it is not the validity but the import of Searle's attempted derivation of an "ought" from an "is" that we need to enquire into. Is the import of such a derivation, supposing it to be valid, simply to reinstate the claims of a natural-law ethics? After all, if the mere facts of the case upon occasion can entail certain moral obligations on our part, would this not be tantamount to treating a moral law or obligation as if it were something prescribed by nature itself?

Not in Searle's eyes. It is really very interesting how, appearances to the contrary notwithstanding, Searle is and remains a consistent linguistic philosopher, never once letting himself be beguiled into ontology or compromised by subscribing to anything on the order of natural laws. True, he insists both that evaluative terms may sometimes be defined in terms of purely factual criteria and that what we ought to do is often determined simply in terms of what is the case; yet all of this he would justify on purely linguistic grounds and without ever once appealing to anything like an ontological basis or foundation for values and moral obligations.

Let us see, though, a little more in detail just how the thing is done. For one thing Searle would have us compare what he calls "the promising game," as that is exemplified in the five propositions above, with any ordinary game, say the game of baseball.[14] In baseball, as Americans so well know, after three strikes a batter is out and is then obligated to leave the field. In such circumstances the batter could not very plausibly argue, "I did indeed strike at the ball three times and miss. But this does not mean that I ought to leave the field. That would be to derive an 'ought' from an 'is.' " Now such a reproach directed at an umpire for his having committed a form of the naturalistic fallacy would hardly be likely to impress anyone, least of all the umpire—at least so Searle

13. Hare himself has written a most telling rejoinder to Searle's article, entitled "The Promising Game," reprinted in Foot, *Theories of Ethics*, pp. 115-27.

14. Searle, "How to Derive 'Ought' from 'Is,' " pp. 112-13; and *Speech Acts*, p. 185.

thinks, and in this even the uncompromising Hare might be forced to agree with him.

More fundamentally, however, what Searle wishes to stress in all of this is that the situation in the promising game is quite like that in baseball. Indeed, that someone's uttering the words "I promise" should under certain circumstances obligate that person to try to carry out his promise rests, Searle thinks, on no more than certain rules, in this case rules of language, or more specifically rules governing the meaning and use of "promise." Similarly, that a baseball player after striking at the ball three times and missing should be obligated to leave the field is again but an affair of rules, not language rules in this case, but baseball rules. Moreover, just as the binding or obligating character of rules in baseball by no means implies that such rules must be on the order of natural law, so also the mere fact that certain linguistic rules authorize the derivation of a moral "ought" from an "is" in no wise entails that such "oughts" must be natural "oughts," or "oughts" determined by anything like natural laws.

Let us look a little more closely at Searle's actual apparatus of explanation in this connection. Borrowing a distinction that was already somewhat current in the literature, Searle would distinguish between what he calls "brute facts" on the one hand and "institutional facts" on the other.[15] Searle considers that "institutional facts," rather than being facts of nature, are facts which quite literally are instituted or constituted by what he calls "constitutive rules"—which rules, in turn, might not improperly be characterized as mere human conventions. Accordingly, in the promising game, no less than in the game of baseball, as Searle himself puts it, "It is a matter of fact that one has certain obligations, commitments, rights, and responsibilities, but it is a matter of institutional, not of brute fact."[16]

What then have we here! Quite clearly it looks as if for all of his talk about the "naturalistic fallacy fallacy" and about deriving an "ought" from an "is," Searle's ethics reveals itself as being not an ethics of natural

15. *Speech Acts,* pp. 50–53.
16. "How to Derive 'Ought' from 'Is,' " p. 112.

norms or natural laws at all, but a mere affair of convention—of νόμος rather than of φύσις. Indeed, let Searle himself spell out these implications of his position in his own words:

> It is perfectly consistent with my account for someone to argue "One ought never to keep promises." Suppose for example a nihilistic anarchist argues that one ought never to keep promises because, e.g., an unseemly concern with obligation impedes self-fulfillment. Such an argument may be silly, but it is not, as far as my account is concerned, logically absurd. To understand this point, we need to make a distinction between what is external and what is internal to the institution of promising. It is internal to the concept of promising that in promising one undertakes an obligation to do something. But whether the entire institution of promising is good or evil, and whether the obligations undertaken in promising are overridden by other outside considerations are questions which are external to the institution itself. The nihilist argument considered above is simply an external attack on the institution of promising. In effect, it says that the obligation to keep a promise is always overridden, because of the alleged evil character of the institution. But it does not deny the point that promises obligate, it only insists that obligations ought not to be fulfilled because of the external consideration of "self-fulfillment."
>
> Nothing in my account commits one to the conservative view that institutions are logically unassailable or to the view that one ought to approve or disapprove this or that institution. The point is merely that when one enters an institutional activity by invoking the rules of the institution one necessarily commits oneself in such and such ways, regardless of whether one approves or disapproves of the institution. In the case of linguistic institutions, like promising (or statement making), the serious utterances of the words commit one in ways that are determined by the meaning of the words.[17]

The Anticlimax of Analytic Ethics:
Is It Any More than a Relativism After All?

With this quotation, then, we conclude our sketch of the structural history of analytic ethics and turn briefly to a bit of stock-taking. Un-

17. *Speech Acts,* pp. 188–89.

doubtedly, the progress of that history has been such as to leave not just its starting points but even its mid-points far behind. Indeed, by the time analytic ethics gets to Searle, Moore's hue and cry against the naturalistic fallacy has long since been quite effectively diverted; the old positivist and emotivist line to the effect that value judgments are but causally determined and hence unreasoned has been pretty thoroughly discredited; and even Hare's characteristic attempt at rehabilitating facts as possible good reasons for ethical and value judgments has presumably been weighed in the balance and found wanting, in that it does not go far enough. Finally, Searle has climaxed it all by making a most telling thrust at that very first of all first principles in analytic ethics, Hume's long-standing injunction against trying to derive an "ought" from an "is."

But what is the import of this progress of analytic ethics, if progress it be? Perhaps, with a certain oversimplification for the sake of concise summation, one might say that the progress has been from a presumed unshakable conviction as to the ultimate separability of fact and value to a new and growing feeling that the two are quite intimately related after all. At the same time, our own use of a natural-law type of ethics as a foil against which analytic ethics might be set forth and exhibited has, we hope, put us in a rather better position to appreciate and assess the achievement of this glorious new-found union of fact and value in which the structural history of analytic ethics would appear to culminate.

What, then, if our appreciation and assessment amounted to no more than a forthright affirmation that such a new-found union of fact and value was no better than a snare and a delusion? That would be only to betray our bias, surely. And yet to say that the union might very well not be quite what it seems would be something to which one could hardly take exception. For just as the original effort to separate values from facts was admittedly an effort to deprive both moral and value judgments of any basis in fact or in nature, so also it might seem that any effort to overcome such a separation must surely be aimed at a reintegration of values into the world of facts and at a reestablishment of moral obligations as obligations that are incumbent upon us by nature. And yet as Searle's work makes abundantly clear, such is not at all the import of the most recent developments in analytic ethics. For while values are once more brought into intimate relation with facts, it is only with institutional facts and not with brute facts (or, to express it rather less invidiously, with the facts of nature) that values are brought into renewed association. And so it is that while "oughts" may indeed be derived from an "is," this is only in virtue of the constitutive rules of an institution like that of promising, and not at all in virtue of any grounding of our obligations in the facts and laws of nature. In other words, the latter-day revolution in analytic ethics—supposing it really to be a revolution—is simply the product of a linguistic analysis and not at all a return or conversion to anything like an ontology.

"But what of it?" you will say. "After all, what difference does it make whether our value judgments and our moral obligations are justified on the basis of institutional facts rather than facts of nature? They have been shown to be susceptible of justification and of reasoned defense, have they not; and so, can they any longer be shuffled off as so many unreasoned and arbitrary expressions of feeling or emotion?"

True enough, and yet what such a defense of this last stage of analytic ethics, as typified in the position of someone like Searle, fails to recognize is that to base ethics on no more than institutional facts is thereby to condemn it to a seemingly ineradicable relativism. As Searle so plaintively protests, he would be the last one to say that institutions are "logically unassailable." Moreover, even as regards his paradigm of the obligations of promise-keeping, Searle insists that it could well be that one ought never to keep one's promises, for the obligation of promise-keeping is but "internal to the institution of promising." Hence one has only to renounce the institution, and one is thereby freed from all obligations internal to that institution.

But what about this business of a renunciation, or correspondingly of an acceptance, of an institution? Surely, it cannot be denied that decisions of this sort in regard to institutions must be on the order of moral or ethical decisions. And yet what sorts of reasons may be adduced in support of judgments to the effect that a given institution ought or ought not to be accepted? On Searle's account, it would seem that the only reasons by which "oughts" may be justified are reasons internal to institutions. Here, though, the only relevant reasons would in the nature of the case have to be external to institutions. Are there, then, just no such reasons at all?

In short, if it is true that the recent history of analytic ethics may be thought to have reached its climax in a dramatic reintegration of values with facts—and yet, after all, a reintegration only with institutional and not with brute facts—then such a climax is no better than an anticlimax. Nor could one say that our latter-day analysts are really so different from the ancient Sophists. For both alike would seem to want to make of ethics a mere matter of convention or of institution, and to confine reasoned ethical discourse simply to questions that are internal to institutions. But no sooner does one do this than all of the really interesting and significant ethical questions immediately become external questions —questions as to the validity and justifiability of the institutions themselves. And if by the terms of one's ethical theory there is no way in which such external questions can be spoken to or rationally investigated, then one's ethics, as Stanley Rosen would say, becomes indistinguishable from nihilism. Is such, then, the upshot of the recent structural history of ethics in the analytic tradition?

A Possible Way Out for Analytic Ethics:
The Transcendental Turn

Nevertheless, before we simply write off recent analytic ethics as amounting to no more than a hopeless nihilism, perhaps we can come up with a proposal by which this general type of ethical theory might to an extent be salvaged. Or perhaps it is not so much a mere proposal of salvage which we are about to put forward as it is a disclosure of one of the deepest, and for that reason largely unrecognized, structural roots of analytic philosophy in general and of analytic ethics in particular. For could it be that many of the recent analytic philosophers have, consciously or unconsciously, followed the lead of Kant and taken what might be called the "transcendental turn" in philosophy? [18]

18. In determining the applicability of this notion of a transcendental turn to both analytic and existentialist ethics, I am greatly indebted to my friend and collaborator, M. S. Gram. See our article, "Philosophy and Ethics," in *The Great Ideas Today, 1970*, ed. Robert M. Hutchins and Mortimer J. Adler (Chicago: Encyclopaedia Britannica, 1970).

It is not our intention and would indeed be beyond our competence to venture out amid the shoals of Kantian scholarship and exegesis. Nor do we mean to imply that any analysts, much less all of them, are Kantians in any strict or literal sense. At the same time, it will scarcely be denied that Kant's First Critique did profess to be and certainly was a kind of new departure in philosophy: it recommended what was in effect a radically new way of doing philosophy. Perhaps, therefore, if we can exhibit at least some of the structural features of this new way of doing philosophy—what we shall loosely call "the transcendental turn" in philosophy—we shall then be in a position to see how any number of contemporary philosophers, from among the existentialists no less than the analysts, might be said to have made something like this so-called transcendental turn. Moreover, once it can be shown that transcendental arguments and modes of justification are by no means alien to the analytic tradition in philosophy, it should then be possible to show how, by availing himself of the transcendental turn specifically in the domain of morals and ethics, an analyst like Searle might well be able to extricate himself from at least some of the ethical-theoretical difficulties in which he would seem to have got himself.

First, though, just what is one to understand by this notion of a transcendental turn in philosophy? For our present purposes there are but two features of the phenomenon which we should like to single out for special attention. First, by availing themselves of the transcendental turn, philosophers have often thought that they could thereby provide themselves with a distinctive means for justifying various of their philosophical first principles. Thus Kant, it will be remembered, at the outset of the First Critique lamented that there seemed to be no adequate evidence either a priori or a posteriori that could serve to make it intelligible just *why* natural events and occurrences necessarily had to have causes, for example, or *why* accidents necessarily had to be accidents of substances. *That* every event must have a cause, or *that* accidents must be accidents of substances, Kant was certain were propositions that were true a priori —i.e., they were universal and necessary. But why they should be so, he could not explain; and faced with this problem, he put forward his transcendental mode of justifying such a priori truths. In brief, this justification amounted almost to a kind of challenge that if the causal principle, for example, were not an a priori principle, i.e., if it were not a universal and necessary feature of the things and events of the natural world, then there just would not be a world at all. That is to say, these a priori principles or pure forms of the understanding were to be justified as being the very conditions of our having any experience in the first place, or of there being any world at all.

When we move on to the second feature of such a transcendental turn, we find that it purports to offer philosophers a most ingenious device for obviating certain kinds of ontological or metaphysical commitment. Thus, by way of illustration, one may say that as Kant viewed the matter, if certain of our philosophical first principles are to be justified simply on the ground that without them there would be no world for us at all, and not even any experience in any proper sense, this could only mean that such principles function as ordering principles. That is to say, it is through such principles, and only through them, that our experience comes to be ordered and structured in such a way as to make it a genuine experience in the first place, as contrasted with a mere "blooming, buzzing, confusion."

However, the consequence of conceiving of philosophical principles as the very principles in terms of which we order and structure our experience is that these principles turn out to be not principles of things as they are in themselves but only principles of things as they are for us and as we experience them. Moreover, the world which we thus come to experience must be acknowledged to be what it is and to have the character that it does have largely in virtue of those ordering principles—those categories or pure forms of the understanding—in terms of which we order it, or in terms of which that same world comes to be ordered and structured, as it were, by us and for us. Indeed, is this not the import of that celebrated passage in the Preface to the second edition of the First Critique, where speaking of scientists of the modern period—Galileo, Torricelli, Stahl—Kant remarks:

They learned that reason has insight only into that which it produces after *a plan of its own,* and that it must not allow itself to be kept, as it were, in nature's leading-strings, but must itself show the way with principles of judgment based upon fixed laws, constraining nature to give answer to questions of *reason's own determining.*[19]

In other words, it is not the independent nature and character of the world that determines the rational judgments that we make about it; rather it is those very plans or conceptual schemes that reason projects upon the world that give to it the character that it has. Accordingly, that second feature of the transcendental turn in philosophy might well be described as a kind of obviating or dispensing with ontology or metaphysics in the more traditional sense of those terms. That is to say, our human knowledge is not a knowledge of things in themselves, or of things as they are independently of the way they appear and present themselves to us. Instead, as Kant would have it, while our knowledge of nature and of the natural world is a knowledge that may rightly be characterized as an "empirical realism," it is nonetheless a realism that is set in an over-all context of "transcendental idealism."[20] Or to put the same point a little differently, our knowledge of nature and of the world is justified not in virtue of its being ontologically grounded in the way things in themselves are, but rather in virtue of its being transcendentally grounded in the way our principles of experience and understanding are set up and given to functioning.

Let this suffice by way of a rough and ready characterization of what we understand by the so-called transcendental turn in philosophy, considered as being at once a transcendental means of justification and a sort of transcendental surrogate for ontology and metaphysics. But what now of the relevance and availability of such a turn, so far as analytic and linguistic philosophy is concerned? Is it so entirely out of keeping with the principles and practice of such a philosophy to avail itself of the resources of such a peculiar turn? Hardly. There are indeed analysts who upon occasion have indicated a certain disposition to invoke something very like a transcendental mode of justification, although this has

---

19. Immanuel Kant, *Critique of Pure Reason,* trans. Norman Kemp Smith (London: Macmillan, 1929), Bxiii; italics added.
20. *Ibid.,* A369–72.

been done rather hesitantly and as if these same analysts might hardly be aware of the full import of what they were proposing.

Thus consider how linguistic analysts are always directing attention to what they call the *uses* of words and expressions in language—particularly ordinary language—insisting that a sensitivity to such uses is indeed the key to philosophic wisdom. As examples, consider some illustrations drawn from Stanley Cavell.[21] He says:

> (1) "We do not say I know . . . unless we mean that we have great confidence. . . ."

or again,

> (2) "When we ask whether an action is voluntary we imply that the action is fishy."

Having made these pronouncements on the uses of "know" and of "voluntary," Cavell proceeds to ask himself just what the source is of that necessity or binding force which such uses would appear to have. For it isn't just a matter of whimsy or of occasional choice that one speaks of knowing something only when one has great confidence. It is rather that one can only use "know" in this way; one is somehow bound to such a use. But why and how is one so bound?

In answer to such a question, Cavell suggests that we let the symbol S stand for either (1) or (2) above. He then proceeds to give the following explanation of that necessity that seems to attach to both (1) and (2):

> When (if) you feel that S is necessarily true, that it is a priori, you will have to explain how a statement which is obviously not analytic *can* be true a priori. . . . When I am impressed with the necessity of statements like S, I am tempted to say that they are categorial—about the concept of an action *überhaupt*. (A normal action is neither expected nor unexpected, neither right nor wrong. . . .) This would account for our feeling of their necessity: they are instances (not of Formal, but) of Transcendental Logic.[22]

21. These illustrations are drawn from Cavell's long essay "Must We Mean What We Say?" which has since been reprinted as the introductory essay of Cavell's book by the same name (New York: Scribner's, 1969).
22. *Ibid.*, p. 13.

So much, then, for Cavell and his somewhat tentative and apologetic resort to a transcendental turn as a means of explaining the necessity or binding force that attaches to certain linguistic uses. Why not, though, attempt a similar maneuver within the domain of ethics? True, it never seems to have occurred even to Kant himself to invoke a transcendental mode of justification for ethical principles, at least not in so many words; and, so far as we know, no linguistic analyst has attempted any such thing either. But why not try it? It might be just the thing to rescue from the toils of relativism and nihilism an ethical position like that of Searle's, which seeks to ground ethics upon fact, and yet upon mere institutional facts rather than the facts of nature.

Could not one even go a step further and read Searle as if he had indeed been groping both for some sort of transcendental mode of justification, to explain why upon occasion an "is" might well be a sufficient reason for an "ought," and for some kind of transcendental surrogate, to do duty for the more old-fashioned kind of ontological or metaphysical basis for ethics? For instance, Searle suggests that the very language of promising implicates us in the language of obligation. One cannot say "I promise" without somehow being caught up in the further admission that one ought to keep that promise. Moreover, Searle would not, presumably, construe this situation in the sense that the act of promising, really and *in rerum natura,* involves one in any sort of a natural obligation. It is simply a case of our language rules being such that a use of the word "promise" implicates us in a subsequent use of words like "obligation" and "ought" in the manner specified. In other words, the contrast between Searle's type of linguistic ethics and the sort of ethics that one might call a natural-law ethic could be pointed up in just this way: as Searle envisages the matter, the fact that the act of promising involves one in an obligation to carry out that promise is not anything that might be said to hold in the very nature of the case (i.e., as determined by natural law), but only something that holds in virtue of certain language rules associated with the institution of promising.

Suppose that right at this juncture one invokes a transcendental mode of justification with respect to the institution of promising and the obligations which it entails. The consequence would be that one would then consider this particular institution—call it the promising game—to be, as it were, ineluctable for human beings. That is to say, a human being could not possibly organize his experience or even structure a world, except in terms of the institution of promising. Then, the promising game would be for us human beings entirely of a piece with what we might call the cause-effect game or the substance-accident game, as these latter were understood by Kant: without such "categories" or "pure forms of the understanding" as the determinants in terms of which our human experience is structured, there simply would not be any experience or any world at all. To follow still further the Kantian pattern that is here projected, one would say that judgments as to our human obligations with respect to such promises as we might make would be in the nature of synthetic a priori truths; and just as synthetic a priori truths involving cause-effect relations are for a Kantian shown to be possible by means of a transcendental mode of justification, in like manner the synthetic a priori truths that would specify our obligations under the promising game could, under our extended Kantian scheme, be shown to be possible by an exactly similar type of transcendental justification.

Searle himself in the passage which we quoted above rather inadvertently but no less decisively ruled out any possibility of such a transcendental justification for that particular institutional fact which he calls the promising game and for the moral obligations that are attendant upon it. Instead, he hastened to protest that the last thing he wanted to be accused of was of subscribing to "the conservative view that institutions are logically unassailable." Indeed, the promising game specifically, he seemed to be saying, is one that we may either agree to play or not, simply by our own choice or decision. But whatever may be the case with the promising game in particular, is it in any way necessary in general for Searle to rule out the possibility that at least some institutional facts involving moral obligations are but patterns of synthetic a priori truths that are justifiable by means of a transcendental type of argument? [23]

23. The point we wish to make here is simply that, whereas for Searle the promising game is presumably a game that we may either choose to play or not, for a strict Kantian the game of the categories is not a game that is open to any such choice. On the contrary, if we did not play the game of the categories, we human beings would have no experience of any kind at all. For this reason, we are saying that in fact Searle does not offer a Kantian type of transcendental justification for

There is a footnote in Searle's earlier article which seems at least to point at such a possibility, although from the context one is inclined to suspect that Searle is scarcely aware of the import of his own hint. In his subsequent book he does not exploit the hint at all, or even repeat it. Be that as it may, here is the footnote that appears on the next to the last page of "How to Derive 'Ought' from 'Is' ":

> Proudhon said: "Property is theft." If one tries to take this as an internal remark it makes no sense. It was intended as an external remark attacking and rejecting the institution of private property. It gets its air of paradox and its force by using terms which are internal to the institution in order to attack the institution.
>
> Standing on the deck of some institutions one can tinker with constitutive rules and even throw some other institutions overboard. But could one throw all institutions overboard (in order perhaps to avoid ever having to derive an "ought" from an "is")? One could not and still engage in those forms of behaviour we consider characteristically human. Suppose Proudhon had added (and tried to live by): "Truth is a lie, marriage is infidelity, language is uncommunicative, law is a crime, and so on with every possible institution." [24]

Perhaps we are reading too much into this footnote of Searle's. But just on the face of it, does it not give one the impression that Searle is somehow stumbling upon a transcendental mode of justification for his ethics almost without knowing it and perhaps even *malgré lui?*

---

his basic ethical categories. Yet would this not be a possible means for him to extricate his own ethical theory from the hopeless relativism into which it apparently ultimately collapses?

24. Searle, "How to Derive 'Ought' from 'Is,' " p. 113.

IV

EXISTENTIALISM:
RELEVANT FEATURES
OF ITS STRUCTURAL HISTORY

~~~~~~

Summaries, Misgivings, and Apologies

In the opening chapter we suggested that the structural histories of phenomenology and existentialism, no less than of analytic philosophy, might be seen to have similar structural roots, at least in matters of ethical theory. Having got through a brief structural history of analytic ethics, it is now time for us to stand and deliver with respect to existentialism.[1] To put it bluntly, is it possible to find features in the development of the latter comparable to what we have found, or presumed, in the former?

So far as analytic ethics is concerned, the structural history of its development would appear to have revealed: (1) an initial determination to repudiate any sort of ontological basis or foundation for ethics; (2) a consequent embarrassment as to whether without such a basis ethical judgments could properly lay claim to being in any way reasoned judgments, or ethics itself to being a rational discipline; (3) an elaborate and

---

1. In this summary account we shall make no attempt at maintaining careful distinctions between the different varieties of existentialists and phenomenologists, any more than we did for the varieties of analysts. Instead, we shall tend, simply for economy of reference, to lump all of the former under the name of "existentialists"—quite without prejudice to Heidegger's or Marcel's well-advertised discomfort at being so labeled.

intricate array and exfoliation of linguistic considerations designed to show how good reasons in ethics might be possible after all, without any appeal having to be made to such ontological supports as natural norms or natural laws. Finally, from our vantage point outside of linguistic analysis we sought to assess this structural history of analytic ethics, first by showing how what we have just designated as step (3) seemed to end in failure, and then by suggesting how such a linguistically grounded ethics might be salvaged after all, simply by resorting to a kind of Kantian transcendental turn, with respect to the very linguistic structure itself of such an ethics.

Is there, then, any parallel to these developments to be found in existentialist ethics? We believe that there is. And yet we must frankly acknowledge at the outset that, given the striking heterogeneity and independence of these philosophical movements, any parallel between them is bound to seem precarious at best. For one thing, to search for common structural roots in two such disparate schools might appear to be a dubious philosophical-historical enterprise to begin with. For another thing, unlike the linguistic analysts, who have carried on a sustained and unremitting examination of specifically ethical-theoretical questions from the very outset of their movement, the existentialists have spoken to questions of ethics, particularly questions of ethical theory, almost as an aside and without really anything in the way of systematic examination and treatment. Besides, as regards the literature of existentialism and existential phenomenology, we must confess to its being much more extensive than we have been able to cover; and to the extent to which we have covered it, we can scarcely claim that our judgments upon it are always sure, to say nothing of true.

Existentialism as a Haven
for Ethical Non-Naturalism and Non-Cognitivism

Such confessed disabilities notwithstanding, let us begin by recalling that initial feature of analytic ethics, namely, its early and continued repudiation of anything like an ontological basis for ethics. Is there then a like structural root in existentialism? Certainly there is. As we saw in that earlier quotation from Kierkegaard, the father of the existentialists declared himself quite unequivocally as wanting to have no truck with any and all appeals to what might be termed a factual basis for ethics, or, to employ a different idiom, with any and all attempts to derive "ought" from "is." It is true that this is not the idiom in which Kierkegaard speaks; and yet he leaves no doubt that where the serious man goes wrong is precisely in trying to find a factual basis for his ethics, such that his moral choices and decisions can thus be free of risk and so come to be based on a sure and secure knowledge of fact. Moreover, that Kierkegaard's early injunction continues to be respected by the existential phenomenologists of today is carefully documented by Olafson in his book *Principles and Persons*.[2]

To give but a few examples, Olafson argues that although there is no recognition in so many words among the existential phenomenologists of G. E. Moore's famous open-question test, they nonetheless repeatedly invoke what is tantamount to such a test in their own philosophical arguments. What Moore was intent upon showing was, in Olafson's words, that "*no* property that a situation might be discovered to have could possibly determine by itself the value of that situation."[3] And this is precisely what the existentialists would insist upon no less emphatically than Moore. Indeed, Olafson deftly shows how the existentialists would carry Moore's open-question argument one step further, to make it cut against Moore himself.[4] For while Moore insisted that no non-natural

2. Frederick A. Olafson, *Principles and Persons: An Ethical Interpretation of Existentialism* (Baltimore: Johns Hopkins Press, 1967). We have relied heavily upon this book in the discussion of existentialism that is here being offered. Apart from its intrinsic excellence, the book is invaluable because it does something that very much needed doing. Given the absence of sustained discussions of ethical theoretical questions by the existentialists themselves, it is most helpful for someone to have pulled together the scattered existentialist teachings on this score, to have justified this assemblage with pertinent quotations, and to have put forward a balanced critical assessment. Of the two other books which have tried to do somewhat the same thing—Hazel E. Barnes, *An Existentialist Ethics* (New York: Alfred A. Knopf, 1967), and Mary Warnock, *Existentialist Ethics* (New York: St. Martin's Press, 1967) —the former is so diffuse and the latter so condensed as not to be of much use, at least for purposes of a properly structural history.

3. Olafson, *Principles and Persons*, p. 127.

4. *Ibid.*, pp. 126 ff.

property such as goodness could ever be inferred from a natural property, he nevertheless did hold that the non-natural property of being right was inferrable from the non-natural property of being good. Thus to know that something, *x,* is good is for Moore a sufficient ground for inferring that it is right to pursue *x* or that one ought to pursue *x.* But for the existentialists, *no* property of a thing, be that property a natural or a non-natural one (assuming for the moment that there can be non-natural properties in the first place), is ever a warrant for a prescription of an *action.* In other words, in their eyes, the logical independence that is pointed up in the open-question argument is not simply an independence of non-natural with respect to natural properties, but more fundamentally an independence of all action-guiding considerations with respect to descriptive or factual properties of any kind. Indeed, if Olafson is right, the existentialists would be the first to applaud the succinct pronouncement of the analyst, Kurt Baier: "A fact by itself is logically compatible with any sort of behavior: it cannot by itself guide a moral agent to do one thing rather than another." [5]

Moreover, much as Moore's naturalistic fallacy, with its attendant open-question test, soon led to the so-called non-cognitivism of the positivists and emotivists, in the case of the existential phenomenologists one might say that theirs was a radical non-cognitivism from the very start. True, the non-cognitivism of the analysts tended to be couched in terms of language: moral predicates and expressions of value were said to have a linguistic force that was not primarily descriptive at all, but rather evaluative, emotive, imperatival, and in general action-guiding. In contrast, the existentialists found evidence for their non-cognitivism not so much in terms of language but from a consideration of the free and active human subject to whom moral and ethical decisions were attributable.[6] As they

5. Kurt Baier, *The Moral Point of View* (Ithaca, N. Y.: Cornell University Press, 1958), p. vi. See to the same effect Sartre, *Being and Nothingness,* trans. Hazel E. Barnes (New York: Philosophical Library, 1956), p. 435: "No factual state whatever it may be . . . is capable by itself of motivating any act whatsoever."

6. Thus Olafson flatly declares in *Principles and Persons:* "Both Heidegger and Sartre emphatically deny that human beings can properly be said to *know* what is morally required of them in a way that is genuinely independent of their own individual choices . . . they repudiate in principle the use of the concepts of truth

saw things, in moral situations the subject acts, decides, ventures, projects, and all of this in such wise that a Kierkegaardian subjectivity immediately becomes the order of the day. In cognitive situations, on the other hand, the subject must be recognized as purely passive with respect to the known objects that are simply there and are what they are independently of the subject and his interests, concerns, and projects.[7] Accordingly, the subjectivity of human moral decisions being thus regarded as something radically incompatible with the objectivity of human factual knowledge and cognition, it is not surprising that the existentialists, on the basis of what might be called their psychological evidence of the human moral situation, should have reached a conclusion quite similar to that of the emotivists and non-cognitivists among the analysts on the basis of their linguistic evidence—the conclusion, namely, that all moral and ethical judgments are to be reckoned as radically non-cognitive.

A Divergency in the Structural Histories
of Existentialist and Analytic Ethics

Granted that the existential phenomenologists no less than the analysts are agreed in renouncing any sort of factual or natural basis for ethics, what about the two succeeding steps which we traced out in the structural history of analytic ethics? Is anything comparable to be found in the development of existentialist ethics?

---

and falsity in moral contexts" (p. 107). And why is it that knowledge and truth, in the traditional sense of these terms, is impossible in moral contexts? Olafson's answer is that for the existentialist "a moral judgment is thus a decisional act, just in the sense that it is conceived as a determination which an individual human being makes for himself and as one for which there is no counterpart *in re*" (pp. 140–41).

7. This must not be taken to mean that existentialists themselves necessarily believe the human subject to be thus passive in cognitive situations. Rather it is simply the existentialists' version of the way traditional Western philosophers have understood the role of the subject in such situations. Indeed, an existentialist of Heideggerian persuasion would insist that a cognitive situation of this sort and in this sense is definitely posterior to and derivative from a much more basic mode of human understanding in which a subject may be said to be "in the truth" in a Kierkegaardian sense.

We venture to suggest that it was only after considerable delay, and even then by way of an extensive detour, that the existentialists got around to moving from step 1 to step 2 of what we earlier characterized as developments in the structural history of analytic ethics. Step 1 was the repudiation of anything like an objective or factual status for moral standards and norms. This step, as we have already seen, was taken early in the game by the existentialists, just as it was by the analysts. Step 2, however, consisted in very little more than an ever growing embarrassment and unease, arising from what appeared to be the inescapably unreasoned character of all morals and ethics as a consequence of the denial of the objectivity of norms and values in step 1. But this particular embarrassment and unease the existentialists were a very long time in coming to feel, and some of them would seem scarcely to feel it even today. However, it is at least superficially understandable why the existentialists should not have been much disturbed over the apparent unreasoned character of all of our moral and value judgments. For from the existentialist standpoint, would not the reasons that we give in support of our evaluations be no less free creations of human subjectivity than values themselves? Thus Sartre, speaking of "the given," asks:

> Are we to understand by this that the given (the in-itself) conditions freedom? Let us look more closely. The given does not *cause* freedom (since it can produce only the given) nor is it the *reason* of freedom (*since all "reason" comes into the world through freedom.*) [8]

8. Sartre, *Being and Nothingness,* pp. 486–87; final italics added. See Olafson's comments in regard to this same issue: "The choices we think of ourselves as making on the basis of a certain analysis of the morally relevant features of a situation are only the visible tip of a much more radical choice which includes that analysis itself. It also means that no feature of any state of affairs can confer on itself the status of being what is called a "good-making consideration" or reason, and that it acquires this status only within the context of the very system of evaluative preferences for which it is supposed to provide some measure of independent support. The force of the existentialist thesis that to treat some feature of an existing situation as a reason is—implicitly at least—to choose or decide that it should be one, is to remind us that once we understand the underivability of our evaluative judgments from anything that could be called a truth (whether necessary or contingent), we have no alternative but to espouse them as our own choices" (*Principles and Persons,* pp. 164–65). It goes without saying that, as thus explicated by Olafson, Sartre's position would

What, then, if any and all attempts to find good reasons in support of our ethical judgments are question-begging? So far from being a vice, in the eyes of the existentialists this is really to be reckoned a virtue, in that it serves to remind us all over again that not just our values but even our reasons for thinking them so are but projections of our ineradicable and inescapable human freedom.

Still, this grave, if not defiant, indifference to anything like truly good reasons in ethics is something that we would suggest not all existentialists have been able to maintain too persistently or even consistently. Instead, some of them have found themselves compelled eventually to take step 2. And no sooner have they done so than they have found themselves up against much the same problem as the analysts: how can good reasons be recognized in morals and ethics, short of a commitment to what we have called an ontology of morals and ethics? There would not appear to be any way out of this problem, short of resorting to something on the order of a transcendental turn, and this might make for a worse predicament than ever.

But we are getting ahead of our story. In fact, instead of telling that story, we are allowing ourselves to indulge in cryptic and dogmatic forecasts as to its outcome. Still, before we can return to the occurrence that is next in order in our proposed structural history of existentialism, step 2, we must first consider a little more in detail just how and why the existentialists seemed to have remained indifferent to step 2 for as long as they did.

Actually, and somewhat ironically, we think the explanation lies in the rather peculiar and distinctive role which the so-called transcendental turn has tended to play in the history of existential phenomenology. For unlike the analysts, who only very lately, and then somewhat gingerly and almost unwittingly, have resorted to the transcendental turn, the phenomenologists have tended to recommend such a turn right at the very outset of their entire philosophical enterprise.[9] But oddly enough, just because

---

seem to have many affinities with a position such as that of R. M. Hare. See our discussion in Chapter II above, esp. pp. 32–36.

9. Unhappily, this assertion will have to remain an undocumented one, largely because the matter is so incredibly complex and difficult. Thus the way in which Husserl might be said to have made the transcendental turn is quite different from

this Kantian type of move was basic to their philosophy as a whole, the existential phenomenologists, somewhat like Kant, seem not to have recognized at first how important this device might be for their ethics in particular.[10] Accordingly, it is just this course of development that we should now like to sketch in very briefly.

The Transcendental Turn
in Existentialism: How It Works

Whereas the starting point in philosophy for the linguistic analysts was ordinary language, for the existentialists it was the ordinary concrete human subject, the actual existing human being—i.e., my own lived existence, and yours, and presumably the other man's as well. Moreover, the gravamen of this concern with the lived, personal existence of the human individual was that throughout much of modern science and philosophy both the freedom and the subjectivity of our human existence had come to be seriously compromised. Rather than as subjects freely choosing, venturing, risking, deciding, committing ourselves, etc., it was

---

that of Heidegger, and Heidegger from Sartre, and Sartre from Merleau-Ponty. Moreover, all of these thinkers, had they been familiar with the term "transcendental turn," would doubtless have denied ever having made it, principally because of their eagerness to press their own claims to philosophical originality and so to differentiate themselves from Kant. Nevertheless, from our discussion of the transcendental turn, as it applies to contemporary existential phenomenologists, it should be clear that we are not laying at their door any very strict or literal Kantianism. Instead, we would merely claim it to be obvious on the face of it that all of these thinkers have resorted to what might loosely be called a transcendental method or way of doing philosophy, as contrasted with the sort of thing one finds in most, if not all, pre-Kantian philosophy.

10. This statement might well be considered historically misleading, if not inaccurate, for there certainly were phenomenologists of the earlier period—e.g., Scheler—who did indeed hold that values were objective in the sense of Husserlian "ideas," and who also made the transcendental turn. Nevertheless, since thinkers like Scheler and Hartmann no longer seem to exercise much influence—at least on contemporary existential phenomenologists—perhaps the statement in the text may be allowed to stand.

as if we had come to be treated by both scientists and philosophers as but so many natural objects whose behavior was completely determined by various natural forces and governed by natural laws. But, say the existentialists, such simply is not the life of an existing, living, human individual at all.

Now if we are not mistaken, it is primarily for the purpose of providing a proper philosophical guarantee for this lived existence of the free human subject, in the face of the supposed "objectification" to which it has everywhere been subject in modern thought, that the existential phenomenologists have had recourse to that characteristically Kantian device of a so-called Copernican revolution in philosophy, or better the device of a transcendental turn in philosophy. Put in the most general terms, the way the device works is simply this: so far from supposing that you and I are but so many objects in nature, existing simply as parts of an objective universe, and so caught up in an all-embracing order of things that determines us and everything else to be what it is, objectively and in itself, and quite independently of anything that you or I may think or do about it, why not recognize that it is almost the other way around? Rather than there being any self-existent objective order of things that determines us human subjects to be as we are,[11] is it not we as subjects who take things to be objects in the first place? That is to say, we constitute them objects by considering and treating them objectively, as over against taking them in some other way. In other words, what the existential phenomenologists would seem set on doing in this connection is simply to avail themselves of that second feature of the transcendental turn which we mentioned in

---

11. Cf. Olafson, *Principles and Persons,* p. 47. Speaking to the question of how the existential phenomenologists react to "the scientific study of the natural world," Olafson says: "Their main argument is that this mode of treatment of natural phenomena not only develops out of the quite different conceptual system. . . . The existentialists' counterargument, in essence, is that this mode of self-objectification [i.e., the scientific one] is one that human beings cannot really carry out in a thoroughgoing and consistent way, and that even when the attempt is made, the more primitive non-deterministic set of concepts reasserts itself. The profound sense of their defense of human freedom is accordingly that of the Kantian argument that human beings are so constituted as to be unable to think of themselves as being causally determined."

the preceding chapter. The objective universe, or what might be called the universe of modern science, is deftly deprived of an ontological or metaphysical status in its own right and is invested with what Kant might have called a mere "empirical reality" as contrasted with a "transcendental ideality."

Thus consider for a moment some of the stock examples. As I think back, say, on the way I spent the last two days, I am immediately reminded of how yesterday was a day that dragged terribly. I was driving from Toronto to Chicago, and the hours upon hours spent at the wheel seemed as if they would never end. Today, in contrast, I find myself at my desk writing at 10 o'clock in the evening and saying to myself that I literally do not know where the time has gone! There were errands to run in the morning; in the afternoon I reworked a chapter that I had written the week before; then checked up on some references and dashed off a few letters just before supper; after supper I glanced over the newspaper, and here it is within a couple of hours of bedtime, and the day seems to have passed in almost no time.

As I reflect upon the matter, quite objectively, it is obviously ridiculous to suppose that the time really went faster today than yesterday, for the passage of time is the same yesterday, today, and tomorrow. Indeed, the hour that I spent yesterday on the highway driving between Ann Arbor and Battle Creek was literally neither longer nor shorter than the hour I spent this afternoon trying to check up on the reasons for the hostility of Pope Paul IV toward Cardinal Pole. How then can I say that the one hour was interminably longer than the other?

Or take the contrast between lived space, as it is sometimes called, and objective physical space. There is, of course, no denying that I do experience things as being far or near, or up or down, or behind or in front of me. Yet, when I stop to think about it, I know that in real physical space nothing is literally above or below, or behind or in front of, anything else. Indeed, it is all quite patently a case of how I take things, or how I regard them, whether I consider them as existing in their objectively measurable physical relationships to each other, or in their immediate and uncritically lived relationships as near or far, above or below, etc. Once again, it is the same sort of difference, upon which Merleau-Ponty remarks, between a professional geographer's description of a particular terrain and my description of those same forests and rivers and fields as being those of the countryside where I was born and in which I grew up.[12]

Thus one can readily begin to see just how Kant's device of a transcendental turn in philosophy works for the existentialist. You and I, as supposedly free existing human subjects, are not really integrated into any absolute objective order of reality that deprives us of our freedom and renders illusory our everyday lived experience as men. Whether the world in which we find ourselves is the objective physical universe of modern science or the lived world of everyday experience—this all depends on us, on how we take things to be, and on how we organize and structure our experience so as to make it an experience of that more or less ordered world which is simply our world.[13] So it is that our world is radically different from the world of the ancient Egyptians; the world of the physicist is very different from that of the artist; and the world of the schizoid or agoraphobe is different from that of the so-called normal man.[14]

12. Maurice Merleau-Ponty, *Phenomenology of Perception,* trans. Colin Smith (New York: Humanities Press, 1962), p. ix.

13. See Merleau-Ponty: "Perception is just that act which creates at a stroke, along with the cluster of data, the meaning which unites them—indeed which not only discovers the meaning *which they have,* but moreover *causes them to have a meaning"* (*ibid.,* p. 36); also "The phenomenological world is not the bringing to explicit expression of a pre-existing being, but the laying down of being. Philosophy is not the reflection of a pre-existing truth, but, like art, the act of bringing truth into being" (*ibid.,* p. xx). For an eloquent, not to say powerful, development of this whole theme, see John Wild, *Existence and the World of Freedom* (Englewood Cliffs, N. J.: Prentice-Hall, 1963), esp. chap. 5.

14. To the historically literate reader this paragraph may have revealed a rather glaring ambiguity in our use of "transcendental turn." Interpreted in a strict and orthodox Kantian way, such a turn can only betoken the use of categories or pure forms of the understanding, in the structuring of our world, which are absolutely invariant and are grounded in a transcendental ego. Interpreted, however, in the looser and more relaxed way that is characteristic of many existential phenomenologists, the transcendental turn may signify no more than that we human beings do ourselves choose the very categories in terms of which we shall structure our world. Such an ambiguity in the expression "transcendental turn," so far from invalidating our main thesis, would appear rather to strengthen it in making it just that much more pliable and adaptable. We shall have more to say about these two different senses of the transcendental turn in Chapter V, below.

It is not essential to interpret this rather high-sounding activity of "world-constitution," [15] which the existentialist would attribute to the human subject or to man, as necessarily involving any sort of thoroughgoing philosophical idealism, whether subjective or absolute. [16] The world which the human subject constitutes for himself is not necessarily anything made up out of whole cloth, and certainly not any literal creation out of nothing, as if the individual human subject were like a veritable Jehovah engaged in the act of genesis. Rather one might utilize in this connection the twin categories of facticity and transcendence in terms of which man's human situation perennially takes shape and can best be understood. [17] For in his existence man is always confronted with what he experiences as simply being there, as brute fact. Yet any such coefficient of facticity in man's situation is never one that he cannot somehow go beyond and transcend, in the sense of its being ever open to countless ways of being understood and to various interpretations and constructions that may be placed upon it. [18] And these same interpretations and constructions that are thus a function of the act of transcendence are themselves but a projection of our own interests and concerns in and through which we give a sense and meaning to our own situation, thereby infusing it with a contributed significance and value.

Perhaps, though, it would be well if we were to let the existentialists speak for themselves on the score of this dialectical interplay of facticity and transcendence which they claim for our human situation and our existence as men. Thus Sartre:

> The decisive argument which is employed by common sense against freedom consists in reminding us of our impotence. Far from being able

15. This is Wild's term; see *Existence and the World of Freedom.*

16. See Merleau-Ponty's very nuanced differentiation of his phenomenology from idealism (*Phenomenology of Perception,* Preface, esp. pp. viii–xi).

17. These terms are borrowed from A. De Waelhens, *La Philosophie et les expériences naturelles* (The Hague: Nijhoff, 1961), chap. 3.

18. See Olafson's quotations from Merleau-Ponty to this effect: "rien ne me détermine du dehors"; "je puis á chaque moment interrompre mes projects . . . (et) commencer autre chose . . . il n 'y a pas de cas ou je suis entièrement pris" (*Principles and Persons,* p. 148, n. 5).

to modify our situation at our whim, we seem to be unable to change ourselves. I am not "free" either to escape the lot of my class, of my nation, of my family, or even to build up my own power or my fortune or to conquer my most insignificant appetites or habits. I am born a worker, a Frenchman, an hereditary syphilitic, or a tubercular. The history of a life, whatever it may be, is the history of a failure. The co-efficient of adversity of things is such that years of patience are necessary to obtain the feeblest result. Again it is necessary "to obey nature in order to command it"; that is, to insert my action into the network of determinism. Much more than he appears "to make himself," man seems "to be made" by climate and the earth, race and class, language, the history of the collectivity of which he is a part, heredity, the individual circumstances of his childhood, acquired habits, the great and small events of his life. . . .

. . . Here certain distinctions ought to be made. Many of the facts set forth by the determinists do not actually deserve to enter into our considerations. In particular the coefficient of adversity in things can not be an argument against our freedom, for it is *by us*—i.e., by the preliminary positing of an end—that this coefficient of adversity arises. A particular crag, which manifests a profound resistance if I wish to displace it, will be on the contrary a valuable aid if I want to climb upon it in order to look over the countryside. In itself—if one can even imagine what the crag can be in itself—it is neutral; that is, it waits to be illuminated by an end in order to manifest itself as adverse or helpful. Again it can manifest itself in one or the other way only within an instrumental-complex which is already established. Without picks and piolets, paths already worn, and a technique of climbing, the crag would be neither easy nor difficult to climb; the question would not be posited, it would not support any relation of any kind with the technique of mountain climbing. Thus although brute things (what Heidegger calls "brute existents") can from the start limit our freedom of action, it is our freedom itself which must first constitute the framework, the technique, and the ends in relation to which they will manifest themselves as limits. Even if the crag is revealed as "too difficult to climb," and if we must give up the ascent, let us note that the crag is revealed as such only because it was originally grasped as "climbable"; it is therefore our freedom which constitutes the limits which it will subsequently encounter.

Of course, even after all these observations, there remains an unnamable and unthinkable *residuum which belongs to the in-itself considered* and which is responsible for the fact that in a world illuminated by our freedom, this particular crag will be more favorable for scaling and that one not. But this *residue* is far from being originally a limit for freedom; in fact, it is thanks to this residue—that is, to the brute in-itself as such—that freedom arises as freedom.[19]

The Ambiguous Locus of Ethics
in Existentialism

And now what about ethics? Having tried to evoke a picture or representation of our human situation as the existentialist sees it, we should be able to determine more precisely just where and how ethical issues become relevant to such a situation. For one thing, through the Kantian device of what we have called a transcendental turn the existentialist feels he has guaranteed to the human subject a certain freedom, even in a sense an absolute freedom. For so far from the subject's being caught up in and determined by an objectively existing world, it is rather the world which is, as it were, constituted and determined by the subject. Moreover, this very process of constitution, being understood as a perpetual transcending and going beyond any relative coefficient of facticity in a person's situation, is really a bestowal of sense and meaning upon that situation by the subject himself—a bestowal which is nothing if not a creative introduction of value and significance into the situation.[20] Clearly, all of this both confirms and accounts for that initial feature which we have already noted an existentialist ethics to have in common with analytic ethics —namely, that values have no sort of factual or ontological status in nature; that the so-called facts of the case never have the slightest relevance one way or another in determining whether something is good or bad, or right or wrong, or worthwhile or worthless; and that any judgment as to the value or disvalue of anything can never be a factual judgment at all, but only an emotive or evaluative one. Still, it ought to be just as clear why, unlike the analysts, the existentialists do not find themselves embarrassed by the apparent inconsistency between the seemingly emotive and non-factual character of ethical terms and the apparent reasoned character of moral discourse.

19. Sartre, *Being and Nothingness*, pp. 481–82.
20. See the earlier quotations from Merleau-Ponty, cited in n. 13 above.

The explanation is that since the free human subject brings value to the world and bestows value upon things, it is precisely this subject that tends to be the primary object of ethical concern, rather than the derivative and somewhat factitious distinctions between right and wrong and good and bad that such a subject projects upon things.[21] For what about these original and originating decisions and resolves and determinations of the subject—how are they to be assessed, and what may one say as to their genuineness and their authenticity? After all, as the existentialists see it, it is precisely you and I and the other man who as free human subjects are responsible for the projection of such personal scales of value and of such social orders as embody our distinctions between right and wrong, and good and bad. What, though, about these very projections that we make—are they made in the manner of the serious man, as Kierkegaard would say, or in bad faith, as Sartre calls it; or are they made courageously and authentically and in full consciousness of the venture and the risk involved and of our own utter and inescapable responsibility for what we are thus resolving and deciding upon?

Indeed, it might not be altogether amiss by way of clarification to re-mark just at this point that the existentialists would appear to suffer from a kind of split personality when it comes to ethics. Given the radical tran-scendental turn which they make at the very outset of their philosophical enterprise, it is almost inevitable that just as they are forever insisting that the subject and his world are strictly correlative, so also is it no less true that the subject and his world tend to be, as it were, located on different levels and strata. True, in one way I am in my world as an integral part of it, and even as one object among others within that world; on the other hand and in another sense, I am not any mere object within the world, simply because I have had a hand in the very constitution of that

21. See Olafson's remarks on Sartre's views to this effect: "The 'world' of every-day experience which my free acts help shape *does* have an evaluative structure and we are often misled into supposing that an antecedently established structure confronts our liberty itself. When Sartre describes freedom as 'un échappement au donné, au fait,' he is signalizing precisely this independence of any such logical com-pulsion, as well as the constitutive role of our freedom in relation to the structures of reasons and ends that emerge from practical deliberation" (*Principles and Persons*, p. 153, n. 14).

world.[22] Thus, as regards moral and ethical distinctions, norms, standards of value, and so on, my everyday lived world is indeed permeated and shot through with evaluations, and yet it is so only because I and other human subjects like me have ordered and structured our world just in terms of these norms and values, so that in this sense we may be said to have projected these same values upon the world.

Where, then, is the proper locus or field of ethics? Is its concern with such values, norms, obligations, etc., as have come to be set up and established in the everyday lived world of which we are so inextricably a part? Or should the concern of ethics be rather with ourselves considered as transcendental subjects [23] that somehow manage to transcend the lived world just in the sense that we are no less than the sources of the values in the world and of the very sense and meaning that the world has for us?

Suppose that the existentialist opts for the former alternative as to what the proper business of ethics is. He will then consider himself to be simply one subject among others within the world, and his attention as a moralist will be directed toward the manifold moral and value distinctions that any and all of us simply encounter within our everyday lived world. What he will be inquiring into will be, among other things, the precise

22. See Merleau-Ponty: "I am, not a 'living creature' nor even a 'man,' nor again even a 'consciousness' endowed with all the characteristics which zoology, social anatomy or inductive psychology recognize in these various products of the natural or historical process—I am the absolute source, my existence does not stem from my antecedents, from my physical and social environment; instead it moves out towards them and sustains them, for I alone bring into being for myself (and therefore into being in the only sense that the word can have for me) the tradition which I elect to carry on, or the horizon whose distance from me would be abolished —since that distance is not one of its properties—if I were not there to scan it with my gaze" (*Phenomenology of Perception,* pp. viii–ix).

23. We employ this term with diffidence and reluctance, knowing full well how many of today's existential phenomenologists want to divest themselves of anything like a "transcendental ego" and all of its works. However, much as one may sympathize with their concern not to be saddled with such an inheritance from Husserl (and Kant), the fact must still be faced up to that any existential phenomenologist must acknowledge some sort of distinction between myself as subject, considered as what Merleau-Ponty calls "the absolute source" (see n. 22 above), and myself recognized as being simply one human subject among others in the world. This distinction we have chosen to flag with the labels "transcendental subject" and "subject-in-the-world," acknowledging that such labels can be misleading.

warrant for such everyday evaluations, and whether proper reasons may be given for the various customary moral judgments and appraisals that we make. Indeed, if it is ethical questions and issues of this sort that the existentialist concerns himself with, then he will quickly find that his questions and concerns are not unlike those of the analytic moral philosophers; and almost before he knows it the existentialist, like the analyst, will be taking step 2.

Thus we suggest that no sooner would existentialists direct their attention to the details of their value-structured world than they would immediately find themselves up against the problem of good reasons in ethics. It would be incumbent upon them, that is to say, to account for the fact that the everyday moral and value judgments that are made in the world do indeed appear to be such as may be supported by good reasons; and the good reasons that are adduced seem over and over again to be no less than appeals to the very facts of the case.

Yet, as we have remarked, the existentialists, unlike the analysts, tend not to take this second step, at least not immediately. The reason is that of the two alternative ways that are open to them as to just what and how they would conceive the proper domain of ethics to be, the existentialists by and large have opted for the second rather than the first. That is to say, rather than concern themselves with the question of ethical distinctions and norms within the world, the existentialists have preferred to shift their attention to the transcendental human subject or subjects to whom the world owes its character and constitutions. Then the instant ethical question becomes one of the authenticity or inauthenticity of those choices and decisions which we, as transcendental subjects, make and as a result of which our world comes to be constituted as it is and to be permeated with such values and value distinctions as are characteristic of it.

Difficulties with an Existentialist Ethics
of Authenticity

Let us have a look at what sort of an affair ethics becomes when its concern shifts from a consideration of the responsibilities of human subjects within the world to a consideration of responsibilities of transcendental subjects for the world. For, if we are not mistaken, it is no less than the difficulties and perplexities of an ethics so conceived that would appear to have led at least some existentialists to take step 2 after all, although seemingly rather surreptitiously and almost in spite of themselves. And little wonder, for no sooner do they take step 2 than they suddenly find themselves up against all of those difficulties in regard to the reasoned character of ethical judgments which we have found to afflict the linguistic analysts.

First, however, let us see what some of the difficulties are that seem to beset any attempt at working out an ethics of the transcendental subject, as contrasted with that of the subject-in-the-world,[24] if we may so term the contrast. For one thing, just what standards are to be appealed to, if one is to judge whether those basic, world-constituting choices of transcendental subjects are to be reckoned authentic choices or inauthentic ones, choices made in good faith or in bad? Clearly, one cannot appeal to such norms and standards of value as one finds in the world, simply because these are no more than the free and arbitrary projections of ourselves as transcendental subjects and hence cannot be invoked as standards by means of which the authenticity or inauthenticity of such projections are to be judged. What is more, even the very business of trying to find objective standards for judging the authenticity of the radical choices that we make as free and transcendental subjects cannot be other than suspect. This would be tantamount to proceeding precisely in the manner of Kierkegaard's serious man. What alternative is there, then, but for the existentialists to consider that the authenticity or inauthenticity of our choices as transcendental subjects must be determined not in terms of what we choose but of how we choose it?[25] And this is scarcely very illuminating for purposes of ethics.

---

24. For the justification of this term, see n. 23 above.

25. Kierkegaard has not hesitated to advocate a position like this, although his recommendations have to do with religious faith rather than with ethics: "When the question of the truth is raised subjectively, reflection is directed subjectively to the nature of the individual's relationship; if only the mode of this relationship is in the truth, the individual is in the truth even if he should happen to be related to what is not true" (*Concluding Unscientific Postscript* [Princeton, N. J.: Princeton University Press, 1944], p. 178).

There is another and even more serious difficulty. Presumably it is not to be denied that basic to any existential ethics of the more usual sort is the radical distinction between choices that are authentic and those that are inauthentic, or those that are in good faith and those in bad. Still, just why and on what grounds must we as human subjects consider that we are obligated to any authenticity in our choices? What, after all, is the source of this obligation? Or if, recognizing myself to be a free, existing human subject, I nevertheless insist that I am under no obligation of any kind with respect to the quality of my choices, just how may I be proved wrong?

To meet this challenge, presumably the existentialist would have no other resource than to analyze all over again the peculiar nature of human freedom, spelling out exactly what it means to be a free being. Thus he might say that a free being is precisely one who, in making his choices and decisions, has nothing that he can appeal to, nothing that he can lean on or fall back on in the way of natural norms or standards, no guidelines of any kind that he can look to.[26] He might even go further, pointing out that man's condition as a free being is a frightening and terrifying one, even an *Angst*-producing one, with the result that few men are willing to face up to the realities of their situation, giving themselves over instead to habits of bad faith and pretending to a veritable knowledge of what they ought to do and be in the manner of the serious man.[27]

---

26. See Sartre, "Existentialism is a Humanism," in *Existentialism from Dostoevsky to Sartre,* ed. Walter Kaufmann (New York: Meridian Books, 1956), pp. 294–95: "The existentialist, on the contrary, finds it extremely embarrassing that God does not exist, for there disappears with Him all possibility of finding values in an intelligible heaven. . . . [Man] cannot find anything to depend upon either within or outside himself. . . . Nor, on the other hand, if God does not exist, are we provided with any values or commands that could legitimize our behavior. Thus we have neither behind us, nor before us in a luminous realm of values, any means of justification or excuse."

27. See Sartre, *ibid.,* p. 307: "One may object: 'But why should he not choose to deceive himself?' I reply that it is not for me to judge him morally, but I define his self-deception as an error. Here one cannot avoid pronouncing a judgment of truth. The self-deception is evidently a falsehood, because it is a dissimulation of man's complete liberty of commitment. Upon this same level, I say that it is also a self-deception if I choose to declare that certain values are incumbent upon me; I am in contradiction with myself if I will these values and at the same time say that

Whatever may be the specific details of this or that existentialist's account of human freedom, the instant question concerns the relevance of any such account to the particular challenge that we are now considering to have been put to the existentialist. The challenge was that the existentialist must show the grounds on which it might be supposed that any human subject was under an obligation—a moral obligation—to make authentic choices. Apparently the answer to this challenge took the form simply of pointing out that man is a free being, and then going on from there to exfoliate just what is involved in such a notion of freedom. Yet how, from the fact that man is free in his choices, is one able to infer that he is therefore under an obligation to make his choices in a certain way? Or, put a little differently, supposing that man is free, why should the mere fact that he is so make it wrong for him to pretend that he is not, or to try to conceal from himself his true condition? Is this not to derive an "ought" or an "ought not" from an "is"? And does this not go diametrically counter to what we have seen was the initial step which the existentialists, no less decisively than the analysts, would appear to make? It was just the step of proclaiming, to borrow Olafson's words, that *"no* property that a situation might be discovered to have could possibly determine by itself the value of that situation." [28] How, then, from the fact that the existentialist fancies that he has discovered that man has the

---

they impose themselves upon me. If anyone says to me, 'And what if I wish to deceive myself?' I answer, 'There is no reason why you should not, but I declare that you are doing so, and that the attitude of strict consistency alone is that of good faith.' Furthermore, I can pronounce a moral judgment. For I declare that freedom, in respect to concrete circumstances, can have no other end and aim but itself; and when once a man has seen that values depend upon himself, in that state of forsakenness he can will only one thing, and that is freedom as the foundation of all values. . . . [This] means that the actions of men of good faith have, as their ultimate significance, the quest of freedom itself as such." It is hard to see this passage as being anything but a most painful exercise in trying to speak out of both sides of the mouth at once. On the one hand, Sartre seems to be saying that although bad faith involves being inconsistent with oneself, one cannot say that there is anything morally wrong with bad faith. He then follows this up by declaring that he can of course pronounce a moral judgment, condemning actions that are in bad faith. This is baffling, to say the least.

28. See n. 3 above.

property of being free [29] can he infer that man is under obligation to make choices in full recognition and acknowledgment of that freedom? Or why, from the fact that a man is free, but tries to hide the fact from his own consciousness, should it be inferred that there is something wrong or morally inauthentic about this? Surely, if the existentialist makes a move of this sort, then his ethics is indeed, if not a natural-law ethics in the usual sense, then at least an ontologically grounded ethics.

A Shift of Ground in Existentialist Ethics

Perhaps it is a bit unfair to tax the existentialist with such a betrayal of his own principles of non-naturalism and non-cognitivism in ethics. The seeming inconsistency or betrayal may arise only as a result of that basically schizoid, or perhaps one ought to say amphibious, character of existential philosophy in general. For as we have already remarked, having made the transcendental turn in philosophy, a certain ambivalence in the existentialist's philosophical enterprise would seem difficult to avoid. Should his philosophical concern be solely with the world as it is for us, or the world as it is constituted by the human subject; or should that concern be directed at trying to transcend the mere phenomenal world, or the world as it is for us, so as to get to the things themselves, or to things as they are in themselves, and particularly to the human subject itself? So far as ethics is concerned, it would seem that if the existentialist or phenomenologist opts for the latter alternative, then his ethics can scarcely avoid being an ontological ethics in the sense we have specified, or perhaps even a naturalistic ethics in a broad sense of that term. But why might not the existentialist opt for the former alternative exclusively, and then his ethical concern would be limited to an investigation of what might be called the moral and ethical dimensions of the lived world,

---

29. To speak of freedom as a property of man is like a red rag to a bull, so far as many existentialists are concerned. However, we are confident that the sense of our argument, taken in its full context, will be readily seen not to turn on this particular mode of expression.

simply as it is for us and as it is constituted by us, and not at all as it is in itself? Under such a limitation, the only values and moral distinctions that the existentialist would then concern himself with would be such as we human beings would have introduced into the world and bestowed upon things. Any such thing as a naturalism in ethics or an ontological basis for ethics would thus be ruled out from the very start.

Nevertheless, if the existentialist did adopt such a policy in matters of ethics, then he would find himself faced with much the same difficulties and pitfalls as we found the analysts to be faced with in their steps 2 and 3. In substance, what we found those difficulties to come to in the case of the analysts was the problem of ethical relativism. Thus if the moral obligation to keep our promises were no more than a function of our playing the language game of promising, then all we would need to do would be to refrain from playing that particular language game, and the attendant duties and obligations would no longer be incumbent upon us.

A precisely similar difficulty, we would suggest, arises, or at least might arise, in an existentialist context. It is a difficulty that is not too easy to document in the existentialist literature, largely because existentialists have tended to avoid or to evade systematic investigations into the foundations of ethics, and particularly of the ethics of man-in-the-world. Indeed, insofar as they have made ethical judgments at all, these have usually had a bearing almost exclusively on questions of the authenticity or inauthenticity of our choices as free and transcendental human subjects. But this, as we have seen, is really to transpose ethical questions from the domain of the lived world and to give them an ontological or metaphysical dimension or import which would only seem to create difficulties for, and to be really somewhat alien to, a properly existential phenomenology, considered just as a phenomenology. In any case, we have deliberately excluded this latter alternative in existentialist ethics from our present consideration.

Not so many years ago, however, there was a book published by a Dutch philosopher which does treat of ethics from the standpoint of existential phenomenology and which quite scrupulously restricts the domain of ethics to such moral laws and standards of value as are relevant to the everyday lived world of human experience. The book is entitled, perhaps somewhat misleadingly, *The Phenomenology of Natural Law*,[30] and its purpose is to show that there are moral standards and moral laws, (although not natural laws in the traditional sense) which have a properly rational foundation, thus are in no wise arbitrary, and hence may be seen to be rightfully binding upon us.[31] In fact, Luijpen begins his book with a consideration not in so many words of the problem of ethical relativism, but rather with the cognate problem of legal positivism. He asks whether questions as to what is just or unjust are, as the legal positivists would have it, only internal to a given legal order and hence cannot properly be asked concerning that legal order itself. Should this be the case, then Luijpen avers that in principle there could be "no human behavior which by its very nature cannot become the content of a legal norm." [32] Moreover, the frightening implications of such a thoroughgoing legal positivism were borne in upon jurists and legal scholars in Hitler's Third Reich, where some of the most reprehensible types of behavior were accepted as legal norms. The positivistically trained jurist could ask only whether something were just or unjust according to the law, but not whether the law itself were just or unjust.

Accordingly, placing this problem of so-called legal positivism in a wider setting, one can readily see how, if on the principles of existentialism all values and all distinctions between right and wrong have their origin simply in the absolutely free resolves of human subjects, then there is nothing to prevent an utter relativism of morals and values as between different subjects. Moreover, supposing that a moral order emanates from no more than the free decrees of certain human subjects, must it not follow that such a moral order is purely an arbitrary one? While it will be easy enough to determine what will be right or wrong or just or unjust according to a given system, the question as to whether that system itself

---

30. William A. Luijpen, *The Phenomenology of Natural Law* (Pittsburgh: Duquesne University Press, 1967).

31. Merleau-Ponty seems to hint at a not altogether dissimilar view in suggesting, as Olafson puts it, that "these 'public' evaluative concepts constitute a kind of *intermonde* between the evaluative indeterminacy of things and the self-conscious evaluative activity of the individual" (*Principles and Persons*, p. 158).

32. Luijen, *Phenomenology of Natural Law*, p. 24.

is just or unjust, right or wrong,[33] cannot be determined and, moreover, cannot even have any real sense or meaning.

How, then, does Luijpen propose to meet this problem of the seeming arbitrariness and inevitable relativism of morals and ethics, considered as being no more than free projections of human subjects? Unhappily, although Luijpen is somewhat specific as to what the actual content would be of a universal ethics binding upon all men, he is by no means specific or clear when it comes to determining the precise grounds on which it may be argued that such an ethics, so far from being a mere arbitrary posit, is something that all men may see to be rationally justified. Nevertheless, we believe that by a certain prodding and pushing Luijpen's ethical recommendations may be brought to the point where, for their proper justification, it becomes obvious that resort must be had to something like the device of the transcendental turn applied specifically to ethics. In other words, just as in the case of analytic ethics we found that a certain ultimate arbitrariness could only be avoided by having recourse to the transcendental turn, so things will turn out much the same way when it comes to a justification of ethical schemes and systems of an existentialist variety.

Let us sketch in very lightly some of the salient features of Luijpen's ethics, so far as its content is concerned. He begins by proclaiming that "human existence is coexistence." This is explained as meaning that "on no level of his existence is man wholly 'alone.' No aspect of being-man is what it is unless other human beings are 'present' in it. The presence of others in my existence implies my being-man is a being-through-others." [34] Just where and how do morals and ethics fit into this picture? Luijpen's answer is, "Justice, conceived as man's willingness to act in accordance with the demands of rights and duties is evidently a mode of co-existing, a mode of being together with others in the world." [35] In other words, human existence being coexistence, justice is that particular mode or

33. For a similar predicament in analytic ethics, one might recall Hare's view that any ethics must ultimately rest on what he calls a "decision of principle" (*The Language of Morals* [Oxford: Clarendon Press, 1952], pp. 68–70).

34. Luijpen, *Phenomenology of Natural Law*, p. 145.

35. *Ibid.*, p. 144.

manner of such coexistence as may be recognized as being "right," "just," "obligatory," etc. More specifically, since the inveterate tendency in all human social relations is for men to treat their fellow men as mere objects, thus doing violence to the freedom, the selfhood, the subjectivity of the other, justice calls precisely for the counteracting of this tendency. "The other's right," Luijpen insists, "is the minimum of my 'yes' to his subjectivity." [36]

Once Again a Transcendental Turn in Ethics

Let this suffice by way of giving the barest flavor of what morality and justice consist in for Luijpen. What is more significant for our purposes is the way in which he would go about justifying the obligatory or binding character of a justice so conceived. To put the issue bluntly, just why should I or anyone else imagine that he is in any way bound to say "Yes" to another's subjectivity? Why not say "No" to it, and be damned!

To this question Luijpen's answer is as interesting as it is unclear. A "yes," he says,

> is called for by my existence as a "having to be for the other," as an "ought" on the level of co-existence. And this "call" is not something coming from without, but is I myself. Thus the other's right is a "natural right," better still, an "essential right," for it is implied in the "nature," the "essence" of co-existence. For the execution of his "having to be for the other" belongs to that through which man is authentically man, hence to his "nature" or "essence." In a certain sense he is not a man if he does not execute it, namely, in the sense that he is not a man *on the level of his authenticity*.[37]

Just what is one to make of these odd-sounding lines? Superficially, and despite the reservation implied by the quotation marks around words like "nature" and "essence," one might imagine that Luijpen was at-

36. *Ibid.*, p. 180.
37. *Ibid.*, pp. 180–81.

tempting to justify moral obligation very much in the manner of a natural-law ethic. Thus it is by an appeal to man's nature or essence—i.e., to what man is—that Luijpen would seem to be attempting to provide a foundation for judgments as to what man ought to be.

Yet this surely cannot be—at least not if Luijpen in any way knows what he is about philosophically. Indeed, as we have emphasized so repeatedly in the foregoing pages, the one thing in particular that existentialist ethics would appear to share with analytic ethics is a determined and sustained repudiation of any and all forms of naturalism in ethics: what is the case ontologically can never afford any basis for assertions as to what ought to be the case morally and ethically. It is true that in virtue of what we have called the amphibious character of existential philosophy in general, the locus of existentialist ethics seems so often to be ambiguous as between two very different domains. Thus is the concern of existentialist ethics with what is authentic or inauthentic as regards the transcendental subject or subject-in-itself? Or is the concern with what is right or wrong, good or bad, authentic or inauthentic with respect to subjects-in-the-world—that is to say, with respect to persons and things in the world as it is for us and as in part constituted by us? Although this may be a somewhat pervasive ambiguity in existentialist ethics generally, it is an ambiguity which Luijpen would seem to be at pains to exclude from his own ethics.

Thus not only is he careful to consistently put quotation marks around "nature" and "essence" as applied to man, but he also says explicitly:

> In the Thomistic conception of natural law the objectivity and reality of natural rights and duties is represented as a "being-in-itself," as being in isolation from the subject-as-*cogito*. Even if the natural rights and duties would not impose themselves on any subject-as-*cogito*, they would still "be." [38]

In contrast, Luijpen's own position is meant to be one in which the concern is not with persons or things as they are in themselves, but only as they are for us and as taken up and integrated in our world:

38. *Ibid.*, p. 191.

We rejected this view of objectivity and reality as being objectivistic. For objectivism, "objective" reality is objective-for-nobody. But objective reality can only be spoken of as objective for somebody.[39]

Given this unequivocal repudiation of any kind of ontological or natural-law basis for ethics, just how can Luijpen show that we human beings are truly and indeed bound by certain obligations of justice? Instead of man's nature as it really is, Luijpen has nothing to go by except the nature of man as it appears and as we constitute it in the world as it is for us. Moreover, there is no way in which even this apparent nature of man can provide any basis for morals and ethics, inasmuch as on existentialist principles there would be no more warrant for deriving an apparent "ought" from an apparent "is" than there is for deriving a real "ought" from a real "is." What other alternative is there, then, for Luijpen but to carry the transcendental turn right into his ethics and to say that in the ordering and constituting and structuring of our human world— i.e., of the world as it is for us as men—we cannot avoid experiencing human existence as simply a coexistence, nor can we avoid associating with this notion of human existence as coexistence the further notion of an inescapable human obligation to see to it that such coexistence is a coexistence in the mode of justice. And what does this amount to on Luijpen's part if not an effort, conscious or unconscious, to avail himself of that first feature of the transcendental turn, as we characterized it in the foregoing chapter? That is to say, he would appear to be trying to justify our being bound by certain moral norms and laws, not on any ontological basis of these being a very part of our nature as men, but rather on the basis of these laws being the very means and conditions through which we order our experience, thereby constituting it a properly human experience in the first place. Moral laws, in other words, rather than being laws of nature, are among the very transcendental conditions of our human world's appearing to us in the way it does and of its having the shape and structure that it does have.

This is not to say that our human moral obligation to work for a just coexistence is in any way derivable from, or something that may be made

39. *Ibid.*

intelligible in terms of, the supposed fact of our human existence being a coexistence. No, for the analogy is quite close here to Kant's way of envisaging his so-called pure concepts of the understanding. For just as the association of any event with a cause is a synthetic one—even though it is no less universal and necessary, and hence in need of a transcendental mode of justification—so also an existentialist like Luijpen might argue that the association of an obligation to justice with the very experience which we have of our own nature as men is likewise a synthetic a priori association—and hence one that calls for a transcendental justification.

We are not sure whether Luijpen actually does make this transcendental turn in his ethics. Yet it would seem that the structural history of existentialist ethics, no less than that of analytic ethics, threatens to end in nihilism, unless these thinkers are willing to avail themselves of an escape route through the transcendental turn. But even though this is their only escape, it is by no means clear that existentialists are generally any more aware of their own plight, much less of their sole means of escaping from it, than are the analysts. Nevertheless, there is a somewhat cryptic, not to say difficult, passage from Luijpen that might just possibly be interpreted as an invocation of the transcendental turn:

> From all this it should be evident that for us real and objective means that which imposes itself as unmistakable upon the subject within the "affirmation of being" that the existent subject-as-*cogito* is. The real and objective is the correlate of this "affirmation of being" that the existent subject-as-*cogito* is; the real and objective is the "true" as the unconcealed and therefore unmistakable for the subject. This "truth" is "brought about" by the "letting be" of the existent subject. It is "brought about," "happens" and "originates" at the "moment" (*Augenblick*) when the subject originates as "affirmation of being." [40]

40. *Ibid.*, p. 192.

V

A TRANSCENDENTAL TURN
IN ETHICS:
A POSSIBLE SOLUTION

In the foregoing chapters we have advanced a thesis that is not only far from popular but scarcely even recognized. In summary, it is the thesis that when moral obligation is regarded not as being ontologically grounded in nature and in natural norms and laws, but rather as grounded either in certain linguistic uses or in the free projects of the human subject, then ethics turns out really not to have any ground at all; and instead of any possibility of moral or ethical justification, one is faced simply with nihilism. While we suggested that both analysts and existentialists were presently standing on the verge of nihilism in their ethics, we also suggested a possible way in which each of these ethical movements might exploit certain more or less hidden resources within their own principles, so as perhaps to obviate such a nihilism. Unfortunately, this latter suggestion will doubtless seem utterly farfetched and wide of the mark. For one thing, what we were identifying as the hidden resource which both analysts and existentialists might fall back on was just the resource that we rather crudely labeled a sort of Kantian transcendental turn in philosophy. And how many analytic philosophers would even recognize that such a philosophical turn is in any way implicit in their philosophical principles? While existential phenomenologists would doubtless acknowledge that their general activity as philosophers did indeed presuppose their making something like an initial transcendental turn in philosophy, they might seriously question the resources and even the pertinence of such a philosophical device, particularly when it comes to ethics. After all, Kant himself, who must certainly be reckoned the originator of what might be called the transcendental mode in philosophizing, would seem not to have considered such a mode to be an apposite or appropriate one in ethics.[1] It would seem, then, that anything like a transcendental turn in ethics is not only a questionable notion in itself, but also one that in fairness could hardly be foisted upon any moral philosophers, be they analysts or existentialists.

What a Transcendental Turn
in Ethics Would Involve

Clearly, then, it behooves us to turn our critical attention to precisely this proposal of a transcendental mode of philosophizing, such as might be carried over into the domain of ethics: just what does it involve, and is it feasible as a possible hedge against ethical nihilism? We have already commented in passing on what such a philosophical transcendentalism is supposed to mean when applied to ethics. It is supposed to mean that

---

1. This statement might well be questioned by Kant scholars. For while it is true that Kant does not in his ethics employ a transcendental deduction under that name, he nonetheless does argue for the adequacy of his theory about ethics on the ground that it explains the possibility of ethical obligation. And would not this be tantamount to a transcendental manner of arguing? Not necessarily. Thus in Chapter III we suggested that the transcendental turn has come to be exploited in such a way as to make possible a denial of any ontological or metaphysical status to such a priori principles as are held to be the very conditions of the possibility of our experience of an ordered world. Yet surely Kant, when he undertakes to explain the possibility of categorical imperatives in terms of what he calls "the Idea of freedom which makes me a member of an intelligible world," would not wish to be interpreted as meaning that my freedom and my membership in the intelligible world are of no metaphysical or ontological import. A man's freedom, as contrasted with his being subject to causal determinations, is not something that is only "empirically real" at the same time that it is "transcendentally ideal."

Of course, this is not to deny that in Kant's eyes a man's freedom as a member of the intelligible world can be known only by practical, and not at all by theoretical, reason. This, however, is a consideration that bears only on the question of our knowledge of an intelligible world, and not necessarily on the metaphysical status of that world.

ethical principles, though neither evident in themselves nor susceptible of any direct rational justification, may nevertheless be justified indirectly on the grounds that they are principles which we simply cannot dispense with in that primordial ordering of our experience which is supposed to turn it into an experience of a world, or which we find to be inextricably woven into the warp and woof of those basic language forms in terms of which we discourse about things and about the world. Thus, to follow a somewhat oversimplified line of illustration, one might say that there is no evidence, either empirical or otherwise, which demonstrates conclusively that we human beings by our very nature as men are subject to moral norms or bound by moral obligations; and yet linguistically it would seem that we could not talk about ourselves as human beings, or phenomenologically we could not be presented with an experience of ourselves in the world, without incorporating moral norms, prescriptions, obligations, etc., into the picture. In other words, while ethics may not be rationally justifiable, so far as we human beings are concerned, it is nonetheless somehow linguistically or phenomenologically inescapable. And so it is, following some such line as this, that a transcendental turn in ethics might be able to guarantee a certain necessity and inescapability of ethical obligation.

The only trouble with such a proposed resource for extricating analysts and existentialists from an ethical nihilism is that none of them seem even to have been conscious of it, much less availed themselves of it. Still, supposing that our analytic or existentialist friends were to do so, is the resource one that would really do the trick? Although it is foolhardy to make predictions as to what can or cannot be done in philosophy, it would nonetheless seem, at least on the face of it, that the chances of successfully achieving a transcendental turn with respect to ethics are but slight indeed.

For one thing, could it actually be shown that there are ethical or moral categories which human beings could not forego the use of, any more than they could presumably forego the use of the regular Kantian categories—e.g., unity, plurality, cause-effect, possibility-impossibility, etc.? After all, whatever reservations one might have as to the particular success of Kant's metaphysical or transcendental deductions, there is at least a certain initial plausibility in supposing that without pure concepts of the understanding, like cause-effect or possibility-impossibility, we would have no experience of a world at all. Could it likewise be argued that without ethical notions or value concepts, like right and wrong or good and bad, experience would be simply impossible; or that value categories, no less than categories of the regular Kantian type, are necessary conditions of an ordered experience of any type? Surely, to demonstrate anything of this sort would place a heavy burden on any transcendental argument that might be devised for the purpose.

We have already had occasion to remark on Searle's rather halfhearted footnote, where he suggests that we could not just throw out all constitutive rules through which the moral import of our social institutions becomes established. We "could not" do this, he says, "and still engage in those forms of behavior we consider characteristically human." [2] Just what is the sense of this "could not" here? Does it mean to suggest simply that human life would be so different as to be almost unrecognizable if no constitutive rules and no moral order of any kind were operative? Or does "could not" mean to suggest that human life, and, for that matter, everything else, would be totally and literally inconceivable without ethical categories, which are, in the strict and precise Kantian sense, categories of the understanding without which there would be no understanding of anything at all? [3] It would seem unlikely, if not impossible, for one to establish a "could not" for ethical categories of the latter sort. And yet it is just this sort of necessity that one would have to establish if one were ever to bring off a transcendental turn in regard to ethics that would bestow upon ethical judgments such universality and necessity as would be requisite for the avoidance of nihilism.

Suppose that the impossible were accomplished and that one did succeed in bringing off some sort of Kantian "deduction" of properly ethical

2. Searle, "How to Derive 'Ought' from 'Is,'" in Philippa Foot, *Theories of Ethics* (New York: Oxford University Press, 1967), p. 113.

3. For us to express ourselves in terms of "understanding" might seem to imply that we had committed ourselves to regarding ethical categories as being descriptive in their function, rather than prescriptive or evaluative. However, any such implication is surely gratuitous, the point being that in making a transcendental turn with respect to ethics, it would be precisely evaluative or prescriptive predicates which, among others, would be necessary conditions of our having any kind of ordered experience at all.

categories. Would this actually succeed in obviating nihilism? Once again, we would think not, and yet we cannot deny that any argument to show this must be in fact a somewhat speculative one.

How Kant Would Justify Moral Laws
by Means other than the Transcendental Turn

Speculative or not, we propose to attempt it. To begin with, it might be instructive to consider how Kant himself might have attempted to meet an issue of this sort. However, we must concede that our interpretation of Kant must be as speculative as our argument, for we cannot vouch for anything like an adequate scholarly warrant for the construction which we are about to place upon Kant's ethics. But whether it is warranted or not as a way of reading Kant's texts, we nevertheless hope that it may prove to be illuminating as a way of pointing up some of the comparatively unnoticed issues of contemporary ethics. We have already remarked on how Kant did not—at least explicitly—invoke a transcendental mode of justification for his own ethics. Instead, in the latter part of the *Groundwork* he raises the question as to what sort of initial and fundamental justification may be given for ethics as such: why should we suppose that anything like a moral law is binding upon us at all? [4] Or in Kant's own words, "But why should I subject myself to this principle [i.e, the categorical imperative] simply as a rational being and in so doing also subject to it every other being endowed with reason?" [5] And a little further on, he adds that "this categorical 'ought' presents us with a synthetic *a priori* proposition." [6] That is to say, when I consider myself simply as a human being in the empirical world, affected by all sorts of sensuous desires, there is nothing about the concept of such a being con-

---

4. Immanuel Kant, *Groundwork of the Metaphysic of Morals,* trans. H. J. Paton (New York: Harper and Row, Torchbooks, 1964), p. 104. All page references to Paton's edition of the *Groundwork* are the numbers appearing in the margin and representing the pagination of the second edition of the work.

5. *Ibid.,* p. 102.

6. *Ibid.,* p. 111.

sidered just as such that explains or makes it intelligible why such a being should also be subject to a moral "ought."

How then does Kant go about showing the possibility of such a synthetic a priori principle in ethics? The principle might be restated so as simply to read: "Human beings are subject to the moral law." Now were this synthetic a priori principle in ethics on all fours with a typical synthetic a priori principle in natural philosophy—say, the causal principle that every event must have a cause—then the expected mode of justification would be a transcendental one. That is to say, since it cannot be determined analytically from a mere consideration of the concept of a natural event that it must have a cause, one therefore has to account for the universality and necessity of such a causal principle on the ground that without it our experience would have no order or structure of any kind. It is only insofar as we order and bring together elements in our experience in terms of cause and effect that we have any experience in the proper sense at all.[7]

Yet such would hardly seem to be the way in which Kant goes about justifying his synthetic a priori principle in ethics. Instead, he suggests that "such synthetic propositions are possible only because two cognitions are bound to one another by their connexion with a third term in which both of them are found. The *positive* concept of freedom furnishes this third term."[8] This would seem to say that in Kant's eyes he has "traced the determinate concept of morality [e.g., the categorical "ought"] back to the Idea of freedom."[9] Yet he immediately hastens to add, "But we have been quite unable to demonstrate freedom as something actual in ourselves and in human nature: we saw merely that we must presuppose it if we wish to conceive a being as rational and as endowed with consciousness of his causality in regard to actions—that is endowed with will."[10]

7. Thus in the *Groundwork* Kant understands "experience" in much the same way as in the First Critique: "The concept of nature is, however, confirmed by experience and must inevitably be presupposed if experience—that is, coherent knowledge of sensible objects in accordance with universal laws—is to be possible" (*ibid.,* p. 114).

8. *Ibid.,* p. 99.

9. *Ibid.,* p. 101.

10. *Ibid.,* pp. 101–2.

Nevertheless, in virtue of his power of reason, Kant thinks, a man, as a rational being, "must regard himself *qua intelligence* (and accordingly not on the side of his lower faculties) as belonging to the intelligible world, not to the sensible one."[11] Hence there are "two points of view from which he can regard himself. . . . He can consider himself *first*— so far as he belongs to the sensible world—to be under laws of nature (heteronomy); and secondly—so far as he belongs to the intelligible world—to be under laws which, being independent of nature, are not empirical but have their grounds in reason alone."[12] Accordingly, he says, "We see now that when we think of ourselves as free, we transfer ourselves into the intelligible world as members and recognize the autonomy of the will together with its consequence—morality; whereas when we think of ourselves as under obligation, we look upon ourselves as belonging to the sensible world and intelligible world at the same time."[13]

How is it, then, that "categorical imperatives are possible"? Apparently, the substance of Kant's answer is that it is "because the Idea of freedom makes me a member of an intelligible world."[14] And what sort of a deduction is this? Presumably, it is not a transcendental deduction at all, at least not in the sense of Kant's First Critique, or in the sense of the transcendental turn as we have interpreted it. It would seem to be no more than an ordinary deduction, by which Kant shows that morality is a direct consequence of a person's being a free, rational being in an intelligible world. Is man, then, such a free being and therefore a being subject to the moral law? To this question, as is well known, Kant insists that theoretical reason can give no answer. Instead, it is only through practical reason that we can know that we are free.

Still, such limits as Kant would thus impose upon theoretical reason, requiring that it be supplemented by practical reason, would seem not at all to affect the logic by which the possibility of our being subject to the moral law is seen to follow from the possibility of our being free beings in an intelligible world. Nor, so far as we have been able to determine, does the logic of such a deduction differ in principle from the logic of

11. *Ibid.,* p. 108.
12. *Ibid,* pp. 108–9.
13. *Ibid.,* p. 110.
14. *Ibid.,* p. 111.

the deduction that any natural-law moralist would employ when he is called upon to provide a justification for ethics. For it is precisely from a consideration of man—of the particular kind of being that man is—that a natural-law moralist thinks that he can show both that man is subject to moral laws and what these laws are. Indeed, it would seem to be just insofar as such so-called moral laws are thought to be derived from the very nature of man that they are called natural laws. It is not only the natural-law moralists who attempt this sort of deduction of ethical principles. The existentialists, as we have already noted, resort to precisely the same sort of logic when they suppose that man's obligation to authentic existence is to be rendered intelligible simply in the light of man's nature [15] as a free and autonomous subject.

It is not too much to say that, however much they may be in disagreement as to the content and subject matter of ethics, there is nonetheless an apparent agreement among Kant, the existentialists, and the natural-law moralists as to the logic of any deduction of moral or ethical principles. Nor would that logic appear to be a transcendental one, or the deduction a transcendental deduction. Indeed, our earlier contention would here appear to be reconfirmed—that while it is only by a transcendental deduction that we are able to account for the universality and necessity of natural laws, it is simply by a straightforward deduction from the nature of a rational being as a free being that Kant feels he must explain "how a moral law can be binding."

A First Reason Why a Transcendental Turn
Will Not Do in Ethics

Why would a transcendental deduction not seem fitting in ethics, whereas for Kant, as for so many other modern philosophers, analysts [16]

---

15. The existentialists would undoubtedly bridle at such a term, and yet we trust that in the preceding chapter we have succeeded in showing how such a notion is both warranted and unavoidable in trying to make clear a certain twist in the logic of existentialist ethical thought. See chapter IV above, esp. pp. 75-77.

16. We are saying this on the assumption that the passages quoted above in Chapter III from Cavell are typical of the thought, even if perhaps not of the words, of many analysts.

and existentialists included, it is our last and only resource when it comes to justifying our knowledge of nature and of the natural world? Naturally, we feel no little diffidence about speaking for Kant in any attempt at answering this question. Perhaps, though, we might make more bold to speak for the analysts and the existentialists. In any case, one might simply ask what difference it makes whether in our knowledge of nature we know things as they are in themselves, or only as appearances—i.e., only as they appear to us and as we take them to be. In contrast, when it is a case of our moral obligations—obligations which in the very nature of the case often go counter to our desires and inclinations and place serious restrictions upon our choices—would we be willing to settle for any appearance of obligation (as contrasted with its reality), however persistent, pervasive, and ineluctable the appearance might be? In short, appearances may suffice well enough in the one case, but hardly in the other, where our very interests and desires and wills are at stake.

Indeed, it is pretty much as Kant himself suggested:

All ideas coming to us apart from our own volition (as do those of the senses) enable us to know objects only as they affect ourselves: what they may be in themselves remains unknown. Consequently, ideas of this kind, even with the greatest effort of attention and clarification brought to bear by understanding, serve only for knowledge of *appearances,* never of *things in themselves.* Once this distinction is made (it may be merely by noting the difference between ideas, given to us from without, we ourselves being passive, and those which we produce entirely from ourselves, and so manifest our own activity), it follows of itself that behind appearances we must admit and assume something else which is not appearance—namely, things in themselves. . . . Even as regards man himself—so far as man is acquainted with himself by inner sensation—he cannot claim to know what he is in himself. For since he does not, so to say, make himself, and since he acquires his concept of self not *a priori* but empirically, it is natural that even about himself he should get information through sense—that is through inner sense—consequently only through the mere appearance of his own nature and through the way in which his consciousness is affected. Yet beyond this character of himself as a subject [17] made up, as it is, of mere appearances

17. Paton, in his edition of the *Groundwork,* notes (p. 142, n. 1 to p. 107) that the word "subject" here means "a subject known—through inner sense—as an *object* of experience."

he must suppose there to be something else which is its ground—namely his Ego as this may be constituted in itself.[18]

Surely, the lesson of this message from Kant is one that no analyst or existentialist is likely to forget; as soon as it is a question of our own volition and of ideas coming to us from our own volition—namely, such things as we want and do not have, and such as we propose and project for ourselves as being what we ourselves need—than we find we can no longer settle for mere appearances. It is thus our very selves that are here at stake—what is really requisite for us and incumbent upon us. For this reason we would venture to predict that even if contemporary analysts and existentialists were to become clearly aware of the nihilism that threatens their ethics, and even if they could be brought to see that the only alternative open to them as a means of staving off such nihilism was a Kantian transcendental turn directly within the domain of ethics itself, this would still not be an option they would probably ever bring themselves to take. In ethics, appearances are no substitute for reality, no matter how desperate the condition of one's own theoretical position.

A Second Reason Why a Transcendental Turn
Will Not Do in Ethics

There is still another reason why we think that contemporary moral philosophers are not likely to opt for any transcendental turn with respect to ethics. However, this new reason may seem even more speculative and questionable than the one that preceded it—simply because it may lead us to embark upon a most fanciful, not to say ad hoc, psychoanalytic diagnosis of the ills of modern intellectual history.

It does not really seem so farfetched to say that the distinctive mark of that history has been an ever increasing fascination with, and glorification of, the absolute freedom and autonomy of the human individual; or if not of the human individual, then perhaps of human society; or if not of human society, then of the elusive and mysterious entity or non-entity which we might call the human spirit or *Geist*. Also, this freedom or

18. *Ibid.*, pp. 105–7.

autonomy has tended to be regarded as a sort of culmination of a long process of liberation in which man has progressively freed himself from a subjection to all externally imposed laws, whether human, natural, or divine, and has come to recognize himself increasingly as a being who is not subject to law but rather is the source of all law. Indeed, one wonders if modern cultural history may not be read as a progressive triumph of autonomy over heteronomy, very much in Kant's sense.

Politically, this would seem to be the lesson of much of modern democracy, at least as it is often conceived, where the people, the party, or the movement become the source of all law, and themselves therefore *legibus soluta*. Technologically, this would seem to be the lesson of modern science, as a result of which man is no longer thought of as having his place in nature and of being obligated to know his place and to keep it; instead, modern man thinks of himself as having the power to make over the very face of nature itself, scarifying it or beautifying it or improving it, simply according to his own conceptions and whims. And epistemologically, this would seem to be the lesson of that radical transcendental turn which marks the course of so much of modern philosophy after Kant, and according to which things as we know them are not as they are in themselves, but merely as they are for us and as we determine them according to our forms of intuition, our categories, our language forms, our intentions, our projects, or what not.

Curiously enough, though, it is this very drive toward autonomy, as perhaps the one most pervasive feature of modern thought and culture, that may well prove to be as decisive in preventing modern philosophers from making the transcendental turn in ethics as it has been conducive to their having made the same turn in philosophy generally. It is not hard to see why this should be so. In philosophy generally the transcendental turn really means that, so far from nature being legislative with respect to man, it is man who has come to be legislative with respect to nature. And so it is that Karl Popper is able to quote Kant with approval when he says, "Our intellect does not draw its laws from nature but imposes its laws upon nature." [19] Moreover, right in our own day philosophers and

19. Karl Popper, *Conjectures and Refutations* (New York: Basic Books, 1962), p. 48.

scientists have tended to go beyond Kant in their drive toward autonomy, even modifying Kant's transcendental turn in a most fundamental respect. Kant felt that the pure forms of intuition and the pure concepts of the understanding, through which our intellect imposes its laws upon nature, were somehow fixed and unchanging—i.e., there could be no experience of any kind save insofar as it comes to be structured through the particular forms of space and time, as well as the particular categories which Kant felt he had been able to derive from the table of judgments. However, the current fashion now in both science and philosophy tends to be to think that although experience is possible only in terms of some a priori conceptual scheme or other, there is no necessary determination as to which particular scheme that must be. On the contrary, conceptual schemes tend to change, one scientific theory displacing another, or one philosophical way of looking at things giving place to an entirely new way of seeing. Indeed, to express this in the way that has come to be somewhat commonplace now: such changes in our basic scientific or philosophical outlook are not to be understood in terms of our coming to see new facts, but rather in terms of our coming to see the facts in a new way.[20]

This currently fashionable variant on Kant's transcendental turn does not tend to compromise in any way that progressive drive toward autonomy which has been so characteristic of modern thought; quite the contrary—it furthers it. Rather than maintaining that our a priori human conceptual scheme, in terms of which we structure our experience, should be something fixed and determinate for all time and for every human subject, the current interpretation of the transcendental turn claims that it is a free projection of the subject, and that the subject is ever free to change and to replace it with some other.[21]

20. This contrast between "seeing new facts" and "seeing facts in a new way" has become something of a favorite commonplace among analytic philosophers. Thus J. O. Urmson employs it in his book *Philosophical Analysis* (Oxford: Clarendon Press, 1956), p. 47, and attributes it to Wisdom. The same contrast appears again in G. Warnock, *English Philosophy Since 1900* (London: Oxford University Press, 1958), p. 137.

21. This difference between what might be called the "transcendental turn," strictly conceived, and the "transcendental turn," loosely conceived, I have discussed

But right here we think we have our proper and adequate reason for feeling that contemporary moral philosophers will not be likely to opt for any transcendental turn in respect to ethics—at least not for any such turn in the strict Kantian sense. In our earlier treatment of both analytic and existentialist ethics we found that both sets of thinkers, each in their respective ways and in terms of their own favored jargon, tended to look upon any scheme of morals or ethics as being internally binding, but externally as something that we would be free to take up or lay aside as we might choose. Thus as Searle would have it, if one plays the language game of promising, then certain moral obligations are incumbent upon one; on the other hand, the language of promising, like any other institutional fact, is something that we may either let ourselves in for or not, the choice being ultimately our own. And likewise for the existentialist, a particular scheme of goods and bads, of rights and wrongs, is but one way of our making sense of our world; it is not a way that we have to adopt, or that we cannot but choose to abide by once we have adopted it. On the contrary, the facticity of any one scheme of values is always something that we can transcend and go beyond to an entirely different set of values, thereby bestowing upon our world a very different sense and meaning.

Now what is this if not an entire way of conceiving and approaching ethics which does indeed involve the transcendental turn, although the transcendental turn not in the strict sense of Kant but rather in that loose sense which respects our autonomy as human beings to a degree Kant never did in his efforts to explain how synthetic judgments a priori are possible? The only trouble is—and this should have emerged from our earlier discussions—that no sooner is ethics conceived and approached in this way than it turns out to be a purely relative matter, incapable of rational justification, and thus doomed ultimately to nihilism. Moreover, if to escape this nihilism one places restrictions upon the transcendental turn, demanding that even in its application to ethics it be carried out in the strict Kantian sense, then one immediately sacrifices that absolute autonomy of the human subject or human person, an autonomy which no modern thinker seems ever quite able to bring himself to renege on.

---

in somewhat more detail and from a different angle in *Two Logics* (Evanston: Northwestern University Press, 1969), esp. chap. 9.

We suspect that any contemporary moral philosopher who found himself directly confronted with a choice of either having to sacrifice an autonomy that is truly *legibus soluta,* or having to confess to a complete intellectual nihilism, would never be able to make the former sort of sacrifice.

VI

SOME PROPOSALS TOWARD
AN ONTOLOGY OF MORALS

The argument of the preceding chapters would seem to point to one conclusion: what is requisite by way of providing a proper foundation for morals and ethics is not any mere investigation of the language of morals, or even a phenomenology of morals, so much as an ontology of morals. The reason for this ultimately comes down to nothing more than a rather elementary consideration: for a judgment to the effect that X is good or right to be warranted, it does not suffice that by our language rules we must call X good or right, or that our subjective dispositions and activities are such that we cannot but experience X as good or right; nothing else will do but that X should be good or right. And there we have it!

Unfortunately, however, the mere recognition that what contemporary ethical theory stands in need of is an ontology of morals does not of itself suffice to indicate just what such an ontology must consist in. Nor do we aspire to any pretension of providing such an ontology in this book. Rather our purpose and procedure will be the more halting and modest one of trying to consider and then to answer some of the stock objections which recent ethical thinkers have directed against any such project as that of an ontology of morals.

Stock Objections
to an Ontological Basis for Ethics

Objections to an ontological basis for ethics tend to be of two sorts, critical and uncritical. As might be expected, the uncritical ones are the more insidious and difficult to deal with. Moreover, what most objections of this sort would seem to boil down to is little more than an ingrained suspicion and even prejudice against anything that smacks of ontology and metaphysics in the more traditional sense. Contemporary phenomenologists, by and large, would seem to be no less free of such suspicion and prejudice than are contemporary linguistic analysts. And what is the result? We suggest that it is simply this: Most contemporary philosophers are not aware of the fact, or, if they were, they would hardly be likely to admit it, that one simply cannot move in today's world of high fashion in philosophy without making something like the transcendental turn. To be cryptically Critical is thus absolutely *de rigueur!* Nor is it just a matter of being cryptically Critical, but also, it would seem, of being uncritically Critical. Thus contemporary philosophers, whether in Oxford or in Paris, have a way of reacting to any and all challenges to the transcendental turn quite in the manner of the little monkeys: they hear no evil, they see no evil, they speak no evil!

Now to all such deep-seated reasons, or non-reasons, for rejecting out of hand any proposed ontology of morals, we have no answer. The past enormities of metaphysics and ontology in the history of Western thought may have warranted a healthy suspicion of their threatened reemergence. But it is only when such suspicion leads to specific objections to specific ontological or metaphysical claims that it is possible to deal with them. As we have already intimated, there are any number of quite legitimate critical objections to a program, such as the one we are proposing for an ontology of morals, that very much need to be met and dealt with. Indeed, these objections would seem to be of the two main sorts that we have already had occasion to mention. Thus, on the one hand, it is objected that ethical properties and ethical distinctions are not of a kind that can have any ontological status in nature or in reality; on the other hand, it is objected that, even supposing such properties to have some sort of onto-logical status in fact, any such factual status of value, so far from pro-viding a foundation for ethics, would simply be irrelevant to it. So for purposes of identification let us call the one sort of objection the *counter-ontological objection,* and the other the *irrelevancy objection.*

The Counter-Ontological Objection
and the Supposed Indefinability of Goodness

We are convinced that the original impetus to the counter-ontological objection came from considerations of the sort that G. E. Moore raised in connection with his elaboration of what he called the naturalistic fallacy. For if such a thing as goodness or value simply could not be equated with or understood in terms of anything in nature or reality, then it is hardly surprising that people should have concluded that goodness could not itself be anything real [1]—that is to say, it could not be an actual feature or property that things in the world could ever literally be said to have or to possess.

Moreover, once it began to appear that goodness might not be a real property of things at all and hence could not have any proper ontological status, it is understandable why philosophers should then have turned their attention to the word "good" and to its "logical grammar." They tried to show how such an expression must have a use in language other than a descriptive use, or invoked the so-called "Fido"-Fido fallacy in order to argue that just because the word "good" is used and used prop-erly in language it must not therefore be supposed that "good" names an entity, goodness, much as "Fido" names Fido. However, all attempts to explain the use of the word "good" linguistically, in such a way as not to involve one in any ontological commitment to the reality of goodness, must surely be thought of as having been subsequent to that more radical

---

1. This was not quite the conclusion that Moore himself drew: from the fact that goodness was supposedly not to be equated with anything in nature or reality, he seems to have concluded not that goodness could not be anything real, but rather that it could only be *sui generis.* See the earlier discussion in Chapter II above.

denial of any ontological status to goodness in the first place, a denial stemming from Moore's naturalistic fallacy argument.

To appreciate the peculiar cogency and import of that argument, it might be well to divest it of some of the rather odd features with which Moore himself had originally invested it.[2] For one thing, he seemed to think of definitions as composites or compounds made up of atomic components, so that when one had analyzed any definition into its component atoms, no one of these atoms in turn could possibly be defined further, for the very reason that it was absolutely simple—literally a simple property or quality. For another thing, not only did these simples have to be indefinable because they were incomposite, but also the very attempt at defining any such simple property could only involve trying to identify it with some other simple property, and this would be tantamount to trying to define the property X in terms of Y, which, being other than X, must therefore be what X is not. Needless to say, any such attempt at definition would be futile, not to say ridiculous. At the same time, given such a notion of definition, the mere fact that a property such as goodness was indefinable would not necessarily mean that it was not real. On the contrary, it could be real just in the manner in which any simple property might be real: its indefinability, in other words, was in no wise a bar to its reality.

Nevertheless, this particular view which Moore had of definition seems not to have played much part in subsequent discussions in the literature of the indefinability of goodness. Instead, the case for such indefinability tended to be made, and almost universally accepted, simply on the basis of the open-question argument. Moreover, the import of this shift of emphasis seems to have been that most moral philosophers of the analytic school tended rather uncritically to assume that because a property like goodness was indefinable it therefore could not be a real or a natural property at all. For suppose that on a more traditional and common-sense view of definition one considers that the purpose of definition is simply to disclose the kind of thing or being it is that one is trying to

2. The comments and criticisms of this paragraph are aimed at some of the things Moore appears to be saying in *Principia Ethica* (Cambridge: At the University Press, 1903), chap. 1, B.

define. In other words, definition is essentially an operation of classifi-
cation—i.e., of bringing the definiendum under one of the main categories or classifications of things in the world, or of things that are real.
Accordingly, if a definiendum—say, goodness—turns out not to be definable at all, this could only mean that it was not classifiable among the
realities of the world and hence could not itself be real, or a real property
of any kind.[3] And so, by such thinking, goodness and value, to say nothing of oughts and ought nots, rights and wrongs, etc., come to be simply
extruded from nature and from reality altogether.

The Open-Question Argument
and Its Refutation

What, then, is the linchpin in this entire association of the indefinability
of goodness with the unreality of goodness? It would seem to be nothing
other than the open-question argument: it is this that clinches the indefinability of goodness, and with it the impossibility of a property such as
goodness ever being reckoned among the ultimate furniture of the world.

The only trouble is that the open-question argument just won't bear
scrutiny! As Moore uses it, it is supposed to involve a kind of test by
means of which one should be able to determine whether any putative
definition that may happen to have been put forward as a definition of
this, that, or the other really is a definition at all. For example, no sooner
does one seek to define goodness, say, in terms of anything whatever, be
it fish or fowl or good red herring, than it can immediately be seen to be
at least open to question whether that is really what goodness is after all.

---

3. Of course, on an Aristotelian scheme of definition such as has been more or
less presupposed in the present paragraph, even if goodness were not subsumable
under any of the *summa genera*, it might still conceivably be either a *summum
genus* in its own right, or possibly one of the "transcendentals" as the Scholastics
were wont to call them. On either of these alternatives the mere fact that goodness
is not to be reckoned under any of the categories would not warrant the conclusion
that goodness could not therefore be anything real. However, so far as we know, an
awareness of either of these two alternatives does not seem to have played much of
a role in such thinking as the post-Moorean philosophers deigned to bestow on the
question of the ontological status of goodness or value.

However, Moore's view of the logic of definition was such that if a putative definition were even so much as open to question, then it could not properly be a definition in the first place. And the reason Moore thought this was that he supposed that any definition must be an analytic truth.[4] However, an analytic truth is one the opposite of which is simply inconceivable because self-contradictory. But for a proposed definition to be open to question means that its opposite is at least conceivable, with the result that the proposed definition turns out not to be analytic, and hence not a definition.

There must be something wrong with this picture. If one thinks of definition in a common-sense way as being nothing but a device for stating what essentially this, that, or the other given thing is, then immediately it becomes clear that there just aren't any definitions in this sense that are not open to question. Indeed, the sorts of things that used to be called real definitions are nothing more nor less than attempts at trying to say what the various things of the world are: "What is man that thou art mindful of him?" or What is the time? or What is the thing which the geologists call a "fault"? Surely, there are no answers to questions of this sort that are not open to question. Thus I may be quite convinced that what man is, is a rational animal. Yet at the same time I must recognize that I might be mistaken. Maybe it isn't necessary that man be rational at all. Or maybe it isn't even necessary to be an animal to be human. Why might not a computerized robot qualify perfectly well as a human being? I need not necessarily give credence to these particular doubts, and yet there is no denying that as doubts they make perfectly good sense. Does this mean, though, that merely because such doubts may be entertained with respect to my definition of man, my purported definition cannot qualify as a definition at all? Of course not.

In fact, we might go so far as to say that any definition that purports to be a real definition is in principle capable of being doubted. For whatever it is in the real world that we may happen to want to know about, in the sense of wanting to know what kind of a thing it is and what per-

---

4. For a more elaborate criticism of the entire conception of definition that is operative in Moore's discussion, see Henry B. Veatch, *Two Logics* (Evanston: Northwestern University Press, 1969), esp. chaps. 3 and 4.

tains to it essentially, it is always possible that what we may have thought to be of the very essence of the thing in question may not really be so at all. Such a possibility is nothing more than a function of our normal fallibility: what we might have taken a given thing to be may not be what it really is. Accordingly, looked at in this light, so far from its being impossible for a definition ever to be open to question, a real definition is always open to question; and, with this, Moore's open-question argument simply collapses.

A Reaffirmation
of the Definability of Goodness and of the Possibility
of Its Having an Ontological Status

Once Moore's open-question test turns out to be no test at all of the validity of definitions, then the mainstay of his entire contention that goodness is in principle indefinable gives way completely. And if goodness thus becomes once again definable, then there is no reason in principle why it should not be defined directly in terms of certain of the features or properties of the real world. In such a case, goodness or value would once more have reentered the land of the living, as it were, as being true flesh-and-blood denizens of the natural world. And indeed, if there really are in the world round things and square, organic things and inorganic, heavy things and light, fast things and slow, why should there not also be good things and bad?[5] Such a value or disvalue as might thus attach to things need not be merely relative to us,[6] or a mere function of the way things appear to us, or the way we take them to be, or the way we talk about them. The value or the disvalue might well pertain to things as they are in themselves, and thus be possessed of a proper ontological

5. This rhetorical question could be somewhat misleading. For, as we shall see presently, even if goodness can be shown to be a real property of things, it cannot be a property like round or green or what not, but rather must be more on the order of a so-called supervenient or consequential property.

6. This seeming denial of any and all relativity, so far as goodness is concerned, will need to be somewhat qualified later.

status[7] of its own. And, with that, exit the positivists, linguistic analysts, and even existentialists! Their respective ethical theories would appear to be simply and suddenly deflated.

Goodness Understood in Terms of Act-Potency

Clearly, though, such purely critical remarks would scarcely appear to have got us very far. Even if the open-question test, contrary to general opinion, does not after all serve to undercut the ontological status of value in any way, this still does not tell us exactly what that status might be. Accordingly, let us make bold to put forward some proposals of our own as to the ontological status of value, relying on some of the more significant insights of what we might loosely term the Aristotelian and the Thomistic ethical traditions. Moreover, since in the recent history of ethics it has been the supposed indefinability of goodness that has been the chief bar to ascribing anything like an ontological status to goodness and value, let us follow the procedure of once more trying to define goodness to see if that will not serve to clarify just what sort of a thing goodness is and what its status in reality might accordingly be.[8]

---

7. Our use of this term in this particular connection may bring to a head reservations which many may have felt all along. For suppose that goodness is not an objective property of things, but rather is dependent upon our liking or our desiring things; would this necessarily mean that goodness could therefore be said to have no ontological status at all? Would not its status be desire-dependent, or mind-dependent, or something of the sort? To this we would but reply that, in inquiring as to the "ontological status" of goodness, we mean to inquire as to the objective and, in this sense, independent status of goodness as it is in the world and apart from us human beings and our feelings and reactions to things.

8. In speaking of defining goodness, we must immediately either withdraw or qualify the term. For so long as we would pretend to be following in the tradition of Aristotle, it must be acknowledged that goodness, so far from being subsumable under any one category or genus, is rather to be found in all the categories, just as being is. But then it is impossible that goodness, any more than being, could ever be defined *per genus et differentiam.*

Even though goodness is in the strict and proper sense indefinable, this still does not preclude Aristotle, or at least Aquinas (see *De Veritate,* Qu. 1, Art. 1, and Qu. 21 and 22), from indicating what sort of a thing goodness is and, in this broad sense,

As a first step toward such a definition of goodness, let us simply recall that in Aristotelian metaphysics and ontology the act-potency distinction is a basic and pervasive category.[9] Things as we know them in the everyday world of common-sense reality are at once universally and radically subject to change: from having been this, a thing becomes that; or being this, a thing is still able to be or become other and different; or not being this, a thing may still have a potentiality to become so. Nor could anything possibly change or become different unless it were able to do so— i.e., unless it had a potentiality for thus becoming and being other and different. Water could hardly come to a boil unless it were able to do so; a child could not learn to walk unless it possessed the necessary capability or capacity for such a thing; nor could a particular gas, say, oxygen, possibly burst into flame unless it were flammable. In other words, it is just such abilities, capacities, and potentialities that are everywhere to be found in our world and that are among the necessary and requisite principles of change.

Further, one readily recognizes that any and all of these potentialities are correlated with actualities. Indeed, "actuality" is no more than a term to designate simply what a given potentiality is a potentiality for; and since any potentiality must be a potentiality, capacity, ability, or capability for something, that something is no more and no less than the actuality of that particular potentiality.[10] Moreover, insofar as I am not actually informed about something or other, but only able to be so; or insofar as the seed is able to sprout and grow and develop into the full-grown plant, but has not actually done so; or insofar as the coiled spring has a potential energy, although there has been no actual release of that energy—in all such cases a potentiality or mere capacity may be compared to the corresponding and correlative actuality, as the imperfect to the

---

from "defining" it. For this reason we think it just as proper to represent Aquinas as insisting upon the definability of goodness as to represent Moore insisting upon its indefinability.

9. Not in Aristotle's sense of "category," of course, but rather in that somewhat broader sense of "category" which has come to be used by many contemporary ontologists.

10. See the Scholastic formula: *potentia dicitur ad actum.* The source materials for this formula, as well as for the argument of the entire paragraph in the text, are to be found in Aristotle's *Metaphysics,* Bk. IX, lls. 1049b3–1050a23.

perfect,[11] the incomplete to the complete, the undeveloped to the developed. It is as if a mere potency just as such somehow bespeaks a certain lack, or imperfection, of which the actuality for its part is simply the fulfillment or completion.

Very well, then, why may not goodness or value be defined or understood as being nothing more nor less than the actual as compared with the potential, and in the very sense of the perfect or complete as compared with the imperfect or incomplete? Note, though, that now that this definition has been proposed, it can no longer be shot down forthwith by simply wheeling out the old blunderbuss open-question argument and firing away in the accustomed manner. All that we need do is to respond by frankly acknowledging that of course such a definition of goodness is open to question. But also open to question is anything and everything else that professes to be a knowledge of what things in the real world are. For whether we want to know what goodness is, or motion or change, or language or logic, or hydrogen or evolution, or what not, all that we can do is to consult our human experience and, by a kind of Aristotelian epagōgē, so familiarize ourselves with what we are seeking to learn the nature of that we eventually come to see what it really is and what pertains to it essentially. And so with goodness or value, no less than with anything else.

Goodness as a Supervenient Property

In addition to appealing to what our experience has evidenced to us in regard to the nature of goodness, we can also take note of how our definition appears to avoid some of the obvious shortcomings that seem to have afflicted other definitions of goodness. For surely, the analysts have been right about one thing: goodness is not a property of things in the usual sense of property at all. To say that a thing is good is not like saying

11. Since the English word "perfect" has come to connote the excellent or the good, it might seem that inasmuch as we are moving toward a definition of goodness in terms of actuality or perfection, our definition is patently circular. However, if "perfect" is taken in its literal sense (cf. the Latin *perficere*) of "complete" or "fulfilled," then any glaring circularity will thereby be removed.

that it is round or square, or pink or blue, or late or early, or above or below. Nor is such a way of understanding goodness faulty simply because it commits the naturalistic fallacy. The analysts themselves came to recognize that, quite apart from the naturalistic fallacy, goodness or value, if a property at all, could not be a property of the usual sort. Instead, it seemed to be what some of the analysts came to call a consequential or supervenient property.[12] That is to say, rather than calling a thing "good" *tout court,* much as we might call it round or pink or what not, we call it "good" *because* it is round or pink or what not; or, better, it is in virtue of the properties that a thing has *tout court* that we judge it to be good. And so goodness turns out to be solely a supervenient or consequential property, and not at all the sort of property that a thing may be said to have *tout court.*

The only trouble is that having clearly recognized that goodness was a supervenient property, the analysts could not then explain how or why it should supervene. That is to say, supposing that a thing may be regarded as good or worthwhile only because of the properties of the more ordinary sort that it has, the analysts, as we have seen, were quite at a loss to explain either the nature or the warrant of this supposed dependence [13] of goodness upon the regular or ordinary properties of the thing. Nevertheless, given a definition of goodness such as the one we are proposing, in terms of a thing's actuality or perfection, it becomes possible to give an intelligible explanation of just how or why the properties of a thing can be the sources of its goodness or value: they are so just insofar as they are properties that evidence the perfection or complete actuality of the thing in question.

Thus, to use some of the stock examples from the literature, a strawberry is said to be a good one, because it is sweet, red, juicy, etc., or a man

12. See Hare's discussion of this, in *The Language of Morals* (Oxford: Clarendon Press, 1952), pp. 80 ff.

13. As we have already sought to show, they tried to construe this dependence as being somehow "logical" or "linguistic"; but since these notions tended to be understood as offering some kind of a substitute for "real" dependence, it was our contention that the analysts must ultimately resort to something like the transcendental turn for the seeming necessary connection between goodness and the properties upon which it supervenes.

is a good man, because he has good judgment, has the courage of his convictions, is fair-minded, etc. And why should being sweet, red, and juicy constitute grounds for calling a strawberry good, or having good judgment, the courage of convictions, etc., be grounds for calling a man good? The answer is that it is precisely the fully developed, perfect strawberry that has such properties; or, analogously, it is only the man of reason and judgment, of courage and justice, who approximates to what a human being might be or could be, and who in this sense has really actualized the full potentialities of being human. In other words, the logic underlying the consequential or supervenient character of goodness or value now becomes clear.[14] Thus a thing is said to be good because it has properties *a, b,* and *c.* And why should *a, b,* and *c* make such a thing good? It is simply because *a, b,* and *c* are characteristics of that thing in its full actuality or perfection, and to be good means to be actual as over against being merely potential. And so it is that our definition of goodness not only takes cognizance of the fact that goodness is anything but a simple property of the ordinary kind, but also makes it intelligible just why and in what sense goodness is a supervenient property.

Goodness as an Objective Property, but One that Bears a Necessary Relation to a Subject

There is another standard, and in many ways eminently plausible, reservation as to the possibility of goodness being but a simple, objective quality or property of things. It is a reservation which not only antedates

---

14. Notice that all we are seeking to do at this stage is to try to straighten out the *logic* of the process known as adducing good reasons in support of evaluations. Thus it is not just *as such* that the properties of being round, red, juicy, etc., are said to be good-making properties in a strawberry; rather it is only *as perfections* or *as actualities* of a strawberry's potentialities that these properties are, as it were, logically fit to serve as good reasons for calling the strawberry a good one. However, if one were then to ask, "But how is one ever to know in a given case that the properties which a thing displays are not mere properties, but rather properties that represent that thing's perfection or actuality?" we must be frank to admit that as yet we have done nothing by way of obviating such *epistemological* difficulties, as contrasted with the mere logical ones.

the specific criticisms of contemporary analysts and existentia.
might even be called a hardy perennial in the history of ethics. ᴀ
highly generalized form, the reservation seems to come down to soᴸ
thing like this: so far from being like other objective properties of things,
goodness and value cannot possibly be simple objective properties of the
object, but must involve some sort of response on the part of the subject,
whether of approving, desiring, commending, liking, applauding, favoring, or what not (or of their opposites in the case of "bad"). Now such a
reservation, stated thus generally, may be readily recognizable as characteristic of a whole gamut of ethical theories: for example, the familiar
varieties of hedonism, where to be good simply means to give pleasure; or
Hume's denial that virtue and vice are matters of fact, it being necessary
first, before qualities such as these are ever to be found, to turn your reflection into your own breast, where you will find sentiments of approba-
tion or disapprobation toward the actions in question; or R. B. Perry's
well-known interest theory of value of a generation ago, in which the
good was held to be simply any object of any interest. These are but a few
examples.[15]

To bring this sort of reservation directly up to date and to give it a
peculiarly contemporary ring, we have only to consider Hare's well-
known criticism of so-called naturalism in ethics.[16] The trouble with
naturalism, he says in effect, is that it seeks to equate goodness with certain natural properties in the object. This will never do, Hare complains,
for it is an inescapable fact of language use that the word "good" is used
to commend. Yet if, when I say that something is a good *A,* I mean no
more than that it is an *A* which is *C* (the *C* here standing for certain
specifiable objective properties of *A*), then it would be simply impossible
for me ever to use "good" as a term for commending an *A* which is *C.*
Thus, to take an example, if to say that for a strawberry to be a good

15. To this distinguished list, Richard Taylor's name may now be added. See his
brilliant and eminently readable book, *Good and Evil: A New Direction* (New
York: Macmillan, 1970). Unfortunately, this book came to our attention only after
the typescript of our own book had already been completed. Hence we have not
been able, in the course of our main argument, to take proper account of this book,
or proper issue with it either!
16. Hare, *Language of Morals,* chap. 5.

strawberry simply means for it to be sweet, red, juicy, etc., then how could I ever commend a strawberry that was thus sweet, red, juicy, etc., as being a good one? For to say that such a strawberry is a good one would be tantamount to saying that a strawberry which is sweet, red, juicy, etc., is a strawberry which is sweet, red, juicy, etc. And this is not at all what we mean to say when we call it good! From this, then, the conclusion is drawn that goodness cannot be an objective property of things, but rather must betoken our subjective response or reaction to such things.

All well and good! Yet in this very connection it is interesting to note that at the opening of the *Nicomachean Ethics* Aristotle flatly declares that the good is that at which all things aim, as if in his very definition of what the good is objectively he was concerned to build right into it a reference to the aims, the desires, or the "objectives" of the subject. In our own attempt at rendering rather more precisely what is involved in this Aristotelian notion of goodness or value, we simply defined the good as being the actual with reference to the potential.

Would not all of this seem to indicate that goodness cannot be considered as the sort of objective property that simply exists there in the object, in splendid isolation from any and all relationships to a subject and to such pro-attitudes as that subject may evince toward that object? Rather it would seem that goodness or value was itself a kind of relational property,[17] just in the sense that it points up the objective properties of the

17. Thus Aquinas flatly says: *Ens enim absolute dicitur, bonum antem in ordine consistat* (*Summa contra Gentiles* III, 20). Moreover, in the *De Veritate* he undertakes to explicate this notion of goodness as being relational by understanding goodness or value as a "transcendental"—that is, a "property" (though these are not Aquinas' terms) that (1) necessarily follows upon being; and (2) "follows upon being considered in relation to another" (see *The Disputed Questions on Truth*, Vol. I, trans. R. W. Mulligan [Chicago: Henry Regnery, 1952], Qu. I, Art. 1, pp. 5-6). Then Aquinas proceeds to explicate this second idea: "The second division is based on the correspondence (*convenientia*) one being has with another. This is possible only if there is something which is such that it agrees with every being. Such a being is the soul, which, as is said in *The Soul*, 'in some ways is all things.' The soul, however, has both knowing and appetitive powers. *Good* expresses the correspondence of being to the appetitive power, for, and so we note in the *Ethics*, the good is 'that which all desire.' *True* expresses the correspondence of being to the knowing power, for all knowing is produced by an assimilation of knower to the thing known" (*ibid.*, p. 6).

object as being themselves the termini of a relation: they are but t.
fillment or actuality of a prior potentiality which was ordered to th
properties just insofar as they constitute the fulfillment or perfection o.
such a potentiality. Indeed, Aquinas even goes so far as to understand
potency or potentiality as a kind of *appetitus* [18]—an appetite or desire for
the relevant perfection or actuality.

Accordingly, on our own attempted adaptation of Aristotle's and Aquinas' account or definition of goodness, no less than on Hare's, goodness
is no mere objective property of things which can both be and be conceived quite apart from such feelings of approval, such pro-attitudes, such
aiming at it, and such tendings toward it as are characteristic of potentialities with respect to their actualities. Thus, recurring to Hare's rather
trivial example of the strawberry, to call a strawberry good is not to
ascribe to it but one more objective property, coordinate with its sweet-
ness, its redness, its juiciness, etc. To call it good is simply to illuminate
these objective properties of the berry in a new light, exhibiting them as

---

18. Although in the passage quoted in the preceding note Aquinas would appear
to confine *appetitus* (appetitive power) simply to animate (be-souled) beings, I
don't believe it amiss to say that he would understand *appetitus* in a fully analogous
sense and so would regard it as being co-extensive with potentiality itself. Thus consider the following passage from *The Disputed Questions on Truth,* Vol. III, trans.
R. W. Schmidt (Chicago: Henry Regnery, 1954), Qu. XXI, Art. 1, p. 7: "A being is
perfective of another . . . also according to the existence which it has in reality
(*secundum esse quod habet in rerum natura*). In this fashion the good is perfective;
for the good is in things, as the Philosopher says. Inasmuch as one being by reason
of its act of existing is such as to perfect and complete another, it stands to that other
as an end. And hence it is that all who rightly define *good* put in its notion something about its status as an end. The Philosopher accordingly says that they excel-
lently defined good who said it is 'that which all things desire.' First of all and principally, therefore, a being capable of perfecting another after the manner of an end
is called good." Clearly in this passage Aquinas is not thinking of "end" in the modern sense, as something that is confined only to human, or at least only to animate,
beings, but rather as something that pervades the entire order of nature and reality,
wherever matter is ordered to form or potency to act (see the "Reply" in Art. 2 immediately following, *ibid,* pp. 10–11). For that matter, for an unambiguous equation
of the notion of end with that of actuality, see *Aristotle's Metaphysics,* trans. H. G.
Apostle (Bloomington: Indiana University Press, 1966), Bk. IX, lls. 1050a7–10: "For
the final cause [or, that for the sake of which] is a principle, and generation
is for the sake of an end; and the end is *actuality,* and potentiality is viewed as
being for the sake of this."

constituting the perfection and fulfillment of what a strawberry might be and could be and, in the non-moral sense, ought to be.

Are Things Good Only Because They Are Desired?

One must not lose sight of what has always been the persistent difficulty from which so many of those ethical theories have suffered that insist upon understanding goodness simply in terms of the responses of the subject—pro-attitudes, desires, aims, approvals, commendations, etc. The difficulty is that in the last analysis one can adduce no more than causes for such pro-attitudes on the part of the subject, and never justifying reasons. And this would be tantamount to reducing one's ethical theory to nihilism.

To point up this difficulty more sharply, suppose that we were once again to pose the ancient question as to whether in one's ethical theory things are held to be good merely because they are desired, or whether they are desired because they are held to be good. If one opts for the former alternative, then there would seem to be no escaping the difficulty that, while one's desires, preferences, and pro-attitudes might be causally explained, ultimately there could be no justifying reasons for them. For why do we give a reason for desiring something or approving it or commending it, if not to show that what we are desiring or approving or commending is somehow good—i.e., it is somehow desirable or appropriate or commendable in itself, and it is for this reason that we desire or approve or commend it, and not the other way around. But with this, we would have forsaken the alternative of supposing that it is only because they are desired that things are held to be good, and would have adopted the opposite alternative of supposing that it is because they are recognized as being objectively good in themselves and in the first place that we then come to desire such things for our part.

Does this mean that, in order for our ethics to be a reasoned one, we must renege on that reservation which we have been considering at such length in these last two sections and presumably applauding—namely, against considering goodness to be a mere objective property of things, existing in absolute independence of any and all subjective responses?

Hopefully, the answer to this question can be "No." And the way to sustain this negative answer is precisely to fall back on that adaptation of the Aristotelian and Thomistic definition of goodness which we are here putting forward. When closely scrutinized, that definition should enable us to avoid the difficulties associated with an overly simple interpretation of the alternative that things are desired because they are good, as well as the difficulties associated with supposing that things are good only because they are desired.

We have already been at pains to show how this definition avoids the difficulties of the former alternative. But how can it avoid the difficulties associated with the usual garden varieties of hedonism, as well as with Hume's theory, or the interest theory, or Hare's theory, or a whole host of others? That is to say, if one cannot even so much as understand goodness, save with reference to what we have termed the subjective factor of desiring, approving, favoring, commending, etc., then how is one to maintain one's ethics as a reasoned one, and not be forced to write it off as a mere nihilism?

To this the answer must surely be along some such lines as these. If one understands goodness as being but the actual as over against the potential, or the perfect toward which the imperfect is ordered, then while goodness is indeed understood as the actual or perfect, precisely insofar as it is desired or aimed at by that which is still only potential, it still does not mean that such actuality and perfection are what they are only by virtue of their being desired or aimed at.[19] And here is just the difference between that account of goodness that is being proposed here, and such other theories as are given to stressing—and up to a point quite rightly so—the relativity of goodness to what we have called the subjective factors of desire, approval, liking, taking pleasure in, etc. In these latter theories the goodness of the object simply consists in, or, better, is actually constituted by, its being desired or liked or approved. On the account we have given, by no stretch of the imagination can one say that the actuality or full flowering of a given potentiality is in any way constituted by or made to be such simply in virtue of the potential being ordered to it or

---

19. See the unequivocal assertion of St. Thomas in *De Veritate*, Qu. XXI, Art. 1: *Bonum enim est in rebus, ut Philosophus dicit.*

tending toward it.[20] After all, while the flourishing of a plant or the excellence of a particular man's character do bear a necessary reference to what a plant or a human being might be or could be, they are not the mere creatures of these relevant potentialities but rather the very norms and standards that are determinative of these potentialities.[21]

By some such means, we wonder if our account of goodness is not one that manages to escape between the horns of the dilemma: goodness as

20. So far from the goodness of a thing being constituted, or actually created or brought into being by the *appetitus* to which it is related, it is well to keep in mind that goodness is to be understood in terms of actuality, and actuality is never in any sense brought into being or constituted by the potency that is ordered to it. On the contrary, as Aquinas sees it, while any potency or potentiality by its very nature is ordered to such actuality as is proper to it, the relation of any actuality to the potency that is ordered to it is not a real relation (*relatio realis*) at all, but only a conceptual relation (*relatio rationis*): "A relation is merely conceptual, according to the Philosopher, when by it something is said to be related which is not dependent upon that to which it is referred, but vice versa; for a relation is a sort of dependence. An example is had in intellectual knowledge and its object, as also in sense and the sensible object. Knowledge depends upon its object, but not the other way about. The relation by which knowledge is referred to its object is accordingly real, but the relation by which the object is referred to the knowledge is only conceptual. According to the Philosopher the object of knowledge is said to be related, not because it is itself referred, but because something else is referred to it. The same holds true of all things which stand to one another as measure and thing measured or as perfective and perfectible" (*Disputed Questions,* Vol. III, p. 6). In other words, to put it rather crudely, just as *the fact* that the table is round, say, is in no wise dependent upon my *knowing* that it is round, so also the *fact* that a certain way of life would be good for me, or perfective or desirable, is in no wise dependent upon my *desiring* it —i.e., my *appetitus* or potentiality being ordered to it.

21. It should be remarked perhaps that many contemporary Thomistic scholars might be inclined to fault this entire effort of ours to utilize for our own purposes St. Thomas' account of the relation of potency to act. For while we insisted in the preceding footnote that in St. Thomas' eyes the relation of act to potency could scarcely be reckoned a real relation, the implication was that he would certainly regard the relation of potency to act as being real. Moreover, since it could hardly be a real relation in the sense of a predicamental relation, it might be presumed to be in the nature of what has sometimes been called a "transcendental relation." Such a presumption, however, would be in disregard of the massive and masterly study by A. Krempel, entitled *La Doctrine de la relation chez Saint Thomas* (Paris: J. Vrin, 1952). Unfortunately, this is neither the occasion, nor could we claim for ourselves the requisite scholarly competence, to assess Krempel's thesis in this regard.

such [22] is neither an objective property that can either be or be understood apart from all reference to such subjective responses to it as desire, approval, commendation, etc.; nor is goodness to be simply equated with our subjective reactions to the object, being itself nothing objective at all.

What about the Irrelevancy Objection?

It may have struck the reader as a little odd that a chapter which opened with a promise to consider two sorts of objections to the claims being made for an ontological status of value—first the counter-ontological objection and second the irrelevancy objection—should have occupied itself exclusively until now with the former, leaving the latter to the very last, when time, space, and patience are all but exhausted. However, we do think that the irrelevancy objection can be given rather short shrift, considering the points that have already been made in connection with the counter-ontological objection.

This irrelevancy objection, as we have already noted, although a favorite resource of the existentialists, is also popular among the linguistic analysts. For as they are wont to put it, moral judgments and value judgments are by their very nature action-guiding; [23] but factual judgments just as such cannot be so, being purely objective. That is to say, in the latter sort of judgment one asserts only what pertains to the object, thus leaving out of account the subject, or such concern as the subject may have with the object, or with what he ought to do about it. For is not "a fact by itself logically compatible with any type of behavior"? [24] Accordingly, since any ethical theory which seeks to give an ontological status to

---

22. This qualification is important, as will become clear in the next chapter. See below, pp. 131–35.

23. See the references to both Baier and Sartre in Chapter IV, n. 5, above. Hare also has put the point most felicitously; see esp. *The Language of Morals*, pp. 29–30. One might add, too, countless references to the same effect in Kierkegaard's *Concluding Unscientific Postscript* (Princeton, N. J.: Princeton University Press, 1941), esp. pp. 118–19, 280–81.

24. This quotation is from Baier. See above, Chapter IV, n. 5.

value must in effect be an attempt to give a factual status to value, such a theory, the analysts seem to feel, is bound to fail. Either it will try to treat facts as if they were values, which they are not and cannot be, not being action-guiding; or else it will somehow manage to turn values into facts, in which case it will then be the values that will have ceased to be action-guiding,[25] being values only in name.

Surely, though, this sort of your-money-or-your-life technique for disposing of even the possibility of an ontological status of value is patently over-simple. As we have already seen, given the definition of value that we have been proposing, the resultant ontological status that values would have is not that of simple properties or of purely objective facts as these are usually understood. Quite the contrary, those values, for all of their being real and objective, are nevertheless values for a subject. Ontologically, that is to say, they are that toward which the subject is oriented and toward which it tends as potency to act. Accordingly, any judgment of value, precisely in its character as a factual judgment, could not be other than action-guiding. Or to put it just a little differently, on this present ontological account of values, facts are values, just to the extent that they are the actualities of certain potentialities; and also values are for their part simply facts, just to the extent that those actions and modes of behavior which are worthwhile and obligatory for us are precisely those toward which we are oriented and at which we aim in the manner of potency to act.

Thus the wisdom that a particular man may have, as well as his sense of justice and his courage and his self-control, are certainly facts; but as facts, they are no less achievements, accomplishments, perfections, which represent but so many actualizations of the man's prior potentialities. And vice versa, suppose that it is incumbent upon a man to make something of himself, to attain some understanding of what is going on, to develop a sense of justice as well as the courage of his convictions—such things represent obligations and standards of conduct which simply as a matter of fact do pertain to human beings and are binding upon us, for

25. See Hare's penetrating remarks about Prichard (*The Language of Morals*, p. 30).

they are just the sorts of actions and modes of behavior to which we are oriented in virtue of our very capacities and potentialities as men.

In short, given such an ontological context of potency and act, doctrinaire statements about how factual judgments cannot be action-guiding, or how action-guiding statements must be non-factual, very quickly lose their force.

In this same connection we might take occasion to comment briefly on the whole business of trying to derive "ought" from "is." To be sure, the irrelevancy objection does not tend to be raised directly in the context of the "is-ought" question; however, since our rejoinder to the former may be extended to cover the latter as well, perhaps we may make some comparatively irrelevant additions to our present consideration of the irrelevancy objection. Briefly we would remark that, much as in that ontology of ethics that we have been advocating, where values can perfectly well be facts, just as facts can be values, so likewise there is no reason why certain obligations may not be obligations in fact, just as, among the relevant facts in the case, would be the fact of our being obliged in certain ways. Nor would such obligations in fact, or facts that entail obligations, involve in their analysis anything more than a recognition that, insofar as certain potentialities are ordered to their appropriate actualities and fulfillments, they are thus ordered and bound to such ends as are thus their proper perfections.[26]

On this basis it will no longer be necessary to worry about deriving "ought" from "is" in either Hume's or Searle's sense. For surely Hare is correct in his criticism of Searle that no "ought" can ever be derived from an "is" unless an evaluative or prescriptive sense has already been incorporated into the key factual premise.[27] At the same time, given the ontological view both of values and of oughts that we are presenting, one does not have to suppose with Hare that the prescriptive aspects of "is"

---

26. Needless to say, such "binding obligations" are ambiguous as between those which pertain to human beings and are thus moral obligations in the proper sense, and those which we might call mere natural tendencies or determinations toward an end.

27. See "The Promising Game," reprinted in Philippa Foot, *Theories of Ethics* (New York: Oxford University Press, 1967), pp. 115–27.

statements can never be gotten out of their descriptive and factual aspects. On the contrary, certain descriptions necessarily involve prescriptions, and prescriptions involve descriptions, and yet without the ones' being reduced to the others in such a way that the descriptions really cease to be prescriptions at all, as the proponents of the irrelevancy objection would wish to maintain.

Is There Anything More to the Irrelevancy Objection?

Have we, though, disposed of the irrelevancy objection in all of its ramifications and implications? One suspects that, at least so far as the existentialists are concerned, the irrelevancy objection involves rather more than a mere insistence that factual judgments cannot be action-guiding. Suppose, for example, that our arguments of the foregoing section are indeed sound, and that we have actually succeeded in showing that there is an entirely legitimate sense in which certain factual judgments may be said to be action-guiding, and certain prescriptions descriptive of our duties and obligations. Would this satisfy an existentialist? Is it not conceivable that he might admit our point and still contend that, even conceding certain factual judgments to be action-guiding, it is but the part of the serious man to seek out such judgments and to rely upon them? Or to put this a little differently, supposing that there could be such things as factual statements of values and of obligations, and that these could not be denied to be action-guiding, is it not conceivable that an existentialist might still regard the kind of action-guiding knowledge that presumably would be incorporated in such statements as being simply irrelevant for ethics?

True, we know of no place in the literature where an existentialist challenge has been posed in just this way. As we have already been at pains to show, it would seem that the starting point of existentialist ethics, no less than of analytic ethics, is just the denial of any factual status to values. Still, supposing an existentialist to forego such a starting point, might he be able to press the irrelevancy objection even so? In suggesting at least a tentative affirmative answer to this question, it occurs to us that one ground on which such an objection might be pressed would be simply the ground of what could be called the content of one's ethics. If we are not mistaken, there are passages in Kierkegaard in which he seems to suggest that human choices may only be considered of moral worth if they are made precisely in the absence of any knowledge of what one ought to do and be, if they are made instead wholly in a spirit of risk, of venture, of blind faith, or what not. In other words, one might interpret such passages in Kierkegaard as not necessarily involving any explicit denial that a knowledge of ethical matters is impossible, but rather that choices made on the basis of such knowledge would simply be of no moral worth.

So interpreted, however, such a line of objection would seem to be rather more an ethical one than an ethical-theoretical one. That is to say, it seems as if Kierkegaard's complaint and objection were based on very little more than the fact that he has a very different conception of what the end or good life for man consists in than does, say, an Aristotle or an Aquinas; and in this sense, so far from denying an ontological status of value, he may be assuming as much and therefore merely disagreeing as to what the character is of this value that is thus conceded to have an ontological status. To meet such an objection, however, would carry us quite beyond the confines of this book.

Still, at the root of Kierkegaard's objection there may be an ethical-theoretical point after all. He may be saying that even if values do have a status in fact and in nature, and even if we can thus come to know what these values are, that would still be a far cry from our acting in accordance with such knowledge; and, after all, the domain of the ethical lies in the sphere of action, not of knowledge. Now, if this is all that the irrelevancy objection amounts to, then the particular point may be conceded, and yet without its being necessary to conclude that such knowledge as we may have of what is in fact morally binding upon us is simply irrelevant to our moral conduct. For in defending an ontology of morals, we would be the first to admit that a mere knowledge of what moral and ethical distinctions are in fact by no means entails that we will act on such knowledge. Indeed, the real moral or ethical problem might be said to arise right at this point: how to bring our choices, and hence our behavior, into line with our moral and ethical knowledge. But the mere fact that in ethics proper the problem is one of choice rather than of knowledge certainly does not imply that knowledge is therefore irrelevant to our moral choices and ethical decisions. This just does not follow.

Perhaps Kierkegaard means something still different by his irrelevancy objection, namely, that such a thing as a genuine knowledge of right and wrong, or of what we ought to do or ought not to do, so far from being irrelevant, might actually be excessively and oppressively relevant—as if the serious man, having a certain knowledge of what he ought to do, could scarcely help doing just that, with the result that there would be no such thing as a problem of moral decision or ethical commitment at all. Now surely it is not this that the existentialist objection comes down to, for if it were then it could be answered in much the way in which Aristotle sought to answer the supposed contention of Socrates that virtue is simply knowledge.[28] In other words, an Aristotelian account of the ontology of morals, so far from entailing the thesis that virtue is knowledge, is supposedly such as to provide the very basis for rebutting that kind of a thesis. Indeed, if this is all that the irrelevancy objection comes down to, then it would seem to be nothing if not irrelevant itself.

We just cannot put down the feeling that once the irrelevancy objection gets beyond its initial point of departure of saying that a knowledge of facts provides no basis for value judgments, then it just doesn't have anywhere further to go.

The Ontological Status of Laws

And now for a brief anticlimax. Since this chapter is concerned with the ontology of morals, it would seem that we ought to speak not just to the ontological status of goodness or value, but to that of natural law as well. In our opening chapter we asserted that for laws to be natural simply means that such things as moral prescriptions and obligations must have a status right in nature. But just how can this be?

Happily, the answer to this question may be developed directly out of

---

28. In an earlier book we have tried to develop what we take it the Aristotelian line of answer would be. See Henry B. Veatch, *Rational Man* (Bloomington: Indiana University Press, 1962), chap. 4.

the ontological structure of potency and act, which, as we have seen, provides the rationale for understanding the ontological status of goodness and value. Of course, when one defines law in terms of the notion of a rule and measure of actions, a distinction would seem to be implied between the source of such a law, in the sense of a law-giver, and the law itself, which thus comes to be given and prescribed.[29] However, when it comes to determining the exact ontological status of laws as they exist and are operative in the real world, we may happily disregard the question of the origin of law—i.e., law as it is the mind of God or of the lawgiver (*in mensurante*)—and confine our attention simply to law as given and hence as it exists in fact and in nature (*in mensurato*). Here the relevant notion is simply that of potency-act, or rather of the fact of a potency's being ordered to its appropriate act. For natural law is nothing but this order of potency to act.

More specifically, of course, one can speak of how an acorn has a potentiality to develop into an oak tree and not a frog, or a tadpole into a frog and not into a man. Or again, so far as men are concerned, one man has a talent for this and another for that, just as all men in their infancy have a potentiality to become mature, intelligent, and responsible adults. But as regards the latter, how many do? Clearly, if a man is to become a mature and responsible adult, there are certain things he must do, certain ways he must go about it; if he neglects these, it will mean that his natural end will not be achieved and his life will be, if not a downright failure, then at least not what it might have been or ought to have been.

Analogously, also, unless a plant has the proper nourishment, or is in the right environment, or is protected against adverse conditions and diseases, it will not develop and flourish as it should. Just as in the case of human beings, where certain conditions, changes, activities, etc., are requisite if a man is to attain his natural end, so also with plants, animals, and natural substances generally. It makes no difference whether these natural laws which thus determine the order of potencies to acts are laws that need to be consciously recognized and acted upon, or whether they be laws that are operative independently of their being known; in either

29. For Aquinas' formulation of this distinction, see *Summa Theologiae* I–II, 90. I, ad I.

case they are nothing other than a natural ordering of potencies to acts, and as such their ontological status is the same.[30] Ontologically, that is to say, natural laws are but rules or measures of actions that specify and determine the order of potentialities to their actualities.

30. *Ibid.*, I–II, 21. 1, where Aquinas remarks: "Debitus autem ordo ad finem secundum aliquam regulam mensuratur: quae quidem regula in his quae secundum naturam agunt est ipsa virtus naturae, quae inclinat in talem finem. Quando ergo actus procedit a virtute naturali secundum naturalem inclinationem in finem, tunc servatur rectitudo in actu. . . . In his vero quae aguntur per voluntatem, regula proxima est ratio humana; regula autem suprema est lex aeterna. Quandocumque ergo actus hominis procedit in finem secundum ordinem rationis et legis aeternae tunc actus est rectus; quando autem ab hac rectitudine obliquatur tunc dicitur peccatum."

VII

TRANSITION
TO AN EPISTEMOLOGY
OF MORALS

▄▄▄

Can Ethics Be an Empirical Science?

Let us suppose for the moment that morals and ethics do have an ontological basis of the sort we have been contending for. Would this not have significant implications with respect to possible ways and means whereby we might hope to arrive at a knowledge of such moral and ethical distinctions? For if distinctions between good and bad, and right and wrong, should turn out to be objective distinctions or distinctions in actual fact, and if moral laws should prove to be on the same footing as natural laws, then surely the implications would be that men could actually observe and learn from experience what they ought to do and how as human beings they ought to act. To use some rather crude analogies, just as we may learn from experience that a straight line is the shortest distance between two points,[1] or that while two events can perfectly well occur at the same time, two things or objects cannot be in the same place at once, so we may also learn from experience that the performances of human beings are not always what they might be or should be, that men

---

1. It is currently fashionable to regard mathematical truths as being no more than analytic or logical truths, and not as truths about the world. Still, we mean to exhibit this axiom of Euclidean geometry as if it were an example of a necessary truth about the world. For this entire notion of truth, as well as for the sense in which such truths may be considered to have an empirical basis, see Henry B. Veatch, *Two Logics* (Evanston: Northwestern University Press, 1969).

are often foolish and perverse in their behavior, just as they can also be upon occasion nothing short of noble and even heroic.

Now if all this is but a matter of experience, something to be learned, would not the upshot be that ethics would thereby have rated a place for itself among the empirical sciences or the sciences of nature—at least if "science" is understood not in the somewhat restricted sense of "modern science" but rather in the broad sense of *scientia,* or knowledge? Yet even with such a qualification it must strike many as paradoxical and even perverse to consider ethics an empirical or natural science. To point the paradox and confirm the perversity even further, need one do more than cite again parts from our earlier quoted passage from Hume:

> But can there be any difficulty in proving, that vice and virtue are not matters of fact, . . . Take any action allow'd to be vicious: Wilful murder, for instance. Examine it in all lights, and see if you can find that matter of fact, or real existence, which you call *vice.* In which-ever way you take it, you find only certain passions, motives, volitions and thoughts. There is no other matter of fact in the case. The vice entirely escapes you, as long as you consider the object.[2]

What could be more damning than this? Indeed, such Humean pronouncements appear so plausible that most of us would unhesitatingly respond that if ethics, to have an ontological basis or basis in nature, must thereby be reckoned among the empirical and natural sciences, then by a straight *modus tollens* argument we would find ourselves constrained to deny even the possibility of an objective, ontological basis for ethics.

All of this notwithstanding, might it not be possible to challenge Hume directly with some counter-examples? Let us consider the following characters of Mr. and Mrs. Bennet as they emerge in the very first chapter of *Pride and Prejudice:*

> It is a truth universally acknowledged, that a single man in possession of a good fortune must be in want of a wife.
> However little known the feelings or views of such a man may be on

2. David Hume, *A Treatise of Human Nature,* ed. L. A. Selby-Bigge (Oxford: Clarendon Press, 1888), pp. 468–69.

his first entering a neighbourhood, this truth is so well fixed in the minds of the surrounding families, that he is considered as the rightful property of some one or other of their daughters.

"My dear Mr. Bennet," said his lady to him one day, "have you heard that Netherfield Park is let at last?"

Mr. Bennet replied that he had not.

"But it is," returned she; "for Mrs. Long has just been here, and she told me all about it."

Mr. Bennet made no answer.

"Do not you want to know who has taken it?" cried his wife impatiently.

"*You* want to tell me, and I have no objection to hearing it."

This was invitation enough.

"Why, my dear, you must know, Mrs. Long says that Netherfield is taken by a young man of large fortune from the north of England; that he came down on Monday in a chaise and four to see the place, and was so much delighted with it, that he agreed with Mr. Morris immediately; that he is to take possession before Michaelmas, and some of his servants are to be in the house by the end of next week."

"What is his name?"

"Bingley."

"Is he married or single?"

"Oh! single, my dear, to be sure! A single man of large fortune; four or five thousand-a-year. What a fine thing for our girls!"

"How so? how can it affect them?"

"My dear Mr. Bennet," replied his wife, "how can you be so tiresome! you must know that I am thinking of his marrying one of them."

"Is that his design in settling here?"

"Design! nonsense, how can you talk so! But it is very likely that he *may* fall in love with one of them, and therefore you must visit him as soon as he comes."

"I see no occasion for that. You and the girls may go, or you may send them by themselves, which perhaps will be still better, for as you are as handsome as any of them, Mr. Bingley might like you the best of the party."

"My dear, you flatter me. I certainly *have* had my share of beauty, but I do not pretend to be anything extraordinary now. When a woman has five grown-up daughters, she ought to give over thinking of her own beauty."

"In such cases, a woman has not often much beauty to think of."

"But, my dear, you must indeed go and see Mr. Bingley when he comes into the neighbourhood."

"It is more than I engage for, I assure you."

"But consider your daughters. Only think what an establishment it would be for one of them. Sir William and Lady Lucas are determined to go, merely on that account, for in general, you know, they visit no newcomers. Indeed you must go, for it will be impossible for *us* to visit him if you do not."

"You are over-scrupulous, surely. I dare say Mr. Bingley will be very glad to see you; and I will send a few lines by you to assure him of my hearty consent to his marrying whichever he chooses of the girls: though I must throw in a good word for my little Lizzy."

"I desire you will do no such thing. Lizzy is not a bit better than the others; and I am sure she is not half so handsome as Jane, nor half so good-humoured as Lydia. But you are always giving *her* the preference."

"They have none of them much to recommend them," replied he; "they are all silly and ignorant, like other girls; but Lizzy has something more of quickness than her sisters."

"Mr. Bennet, how can you abuse your own children in such a way! You take delight in vexing me. You have no compassion on my poor nerves."

"You mistake me, my dear. I have a high respect for your nerves. They are my old friends. I have heard you mention them with consideration these twenty years at least."

"Ah! you do not know what I suffer."

"But I hope you will get over it, and live to see many young men of four thousand a-year come into the neighbourhood."

"It will be no use to us, if twenty such should come, since you will not visit them."

"Depend upon it, my dear, that when there are twenty, I will visit them all." [3]

From this interchange who of Jane Austen's readers would not have it borne in upon him just what were some of the weaknesses, to say nothing of strengths, of both Mr. and Mrs. Bennet? Indeed, the author seems to do little more than to articulate what is already obvious, when she adds as the concluding paragraph of the chapter:

Mr. Bennet was so odd a mixture of quick parts, sarcastic humour, re-serve, and caprice, that the experience of three-and-twenty years had been

3. Jane Austen, *Pride and Prejudice* (New York: Frank S. Holby, 1906), pp. 3-6.

insufficient to make his wife understand his character. *Her* mind was less difficult to develop. She was a woman of mean understanding, little information, and uncertain temper. When she was discontented, she fancied herself nervous. The business of her life was to get her daughters married; its solace was visiting and news.[4]

Now in the light of examples such as this, why not put it to Hume: Who can possibly contemplate the character of a Mrs. Bennet, say, without immediately recognizing that she was indeed, and simply as a matter of fact, a shallow, foolish woman! And how could you, David Hume, possibly maintain that Mrs. Bennet's shortcomings were simply not there in the woman herself at all, as if they were not palpable and obvious for all to see and feel?

Take another example, this time of a very different sort of character and drawn from a very different source. For who is not familiar with that "tale of the courts" which Socrates relates of himself in the *Apology:*

Let me relate to you a passage of my own life which will prove to you that I should never have yielded to injustice from any fear of death, and that "as I should have refused to yield" I must have died at once. I will tell you a tale of the courts, not very interesting perhaps, but nevertheless true. The only office of state which I ever held, O men of Athens, was that of senator: the tribe Antiochis, which is my tribe, had the presidency at the trial of the generals who had not taken up the bodies of the slain after the battle of Arginusae; and you proposed to try them in a body, contrary to law, as you all thought afterwards; but at the time I was the only one of the Prytanes who was opposed to the illegality, and I gave my vote against you; and when the orators threatened to impeach and arrest me, and you called and shouted, I made up my mind that I would run the risk, having law and justice with me, rather than take part in your injustice because I feared imprisonment and death. This happened in the days of the democracy. But when the oligarchy of the Thirty was in power, they sent for me and four others into the rotunda, and bade us bring Leon the Salaminian from Salamis, as they wanted to put him to death. This was a specimen of the sort of commands which they were always giving with the view of implicating as many as possible in their crimes; and then I showed, not in word only but in deed, that,

4. *Ibid.,* pp. 6–7.

if I may be allowed to use such an expression, I cared not a straw for death, and that my great and only care was lest I should do an unrighteous or unholy thing. For the strong arm of that oppressive power did not frighten me into doing wrong; and when we came out of the rotunda the other four went to Salamis and fetched Leon, but I went quietly home. For which I might have lost my life, had not the power of the Thirty shortly afterwards come to an end. And many will witness to my words.[5]

Now surely no one can consider this account which Socrates gives of his own behavior without recognizing that here was indeed a man of no ordinary worth—brave, but without being in the least ostentatious about it; and with a real sense of justice, from which he was not to be deterred by either threats or blandishments, be they from the Left or from the Right. How then could Hume possibly maintain that you have but to consider a man like Socrates, admitted to be virtuous, to examine his character and behavior in all lights, and you will find that his virtue entirely escapes you? Could it be that Hume was somehow strangely value-blind, or, perhaps, virtue-blind? Or must we not rather explain it by saying that when Hume claimed simply to look at the facts and to find no values in them, he was but displaying what we might call a sort of proofreader's mentality? It's as if he had so trained himself as to be able to read letters, words, and sentences, but without heeding the sense or meaning of what is being said at all. Not that such sense and meaning are not there; instead, it's just that the proofreader in reading an author has no particular eye for the sense, but only for the typographical errors. And so analogously, when Hume insists that, in examining an action admitted to be virtuous or vicious, such virtue and vice entirely escape him, this surely betokens no more than that Hume has no eye for values, not that such values are not really there in the facts at all.[6]

5. Plato, *Euthyphro, Crito, Apology, and Symposium,* trans. Benjamin Jowett, rev. Moses Hadas (Chicago: Henry Regnery, Gateway Edition, 1953), pp. 44–45.
6. In the strictures which we level against Hume throughout this section, we are not pretending to anything like a thoroughgoing criticism of his ethical position as a whole. Instead, we are concentrating on but a single point and directing our fire only to Hume's notion that in order to discover distinctions between good and bad, and right and wrong, we must look not to the facts but solely within our own breasts to find such distinctions.

How Is This Moral Blindness to Be Accounted For?

Still, it scarcely suffices, by way of a rebuttal of Hume, to fall back on what amounts to little more than a metaphor and to accuse him of being afflicted with a proofreader's mentality. We need to further explain what it is that tends to bring on this peculiar kind of blindness, and why it should have become so widespread in the present day as to seem perfectly natural and not really a blindness at all. Happily, such an explanation lies ready at hand in that same ontological account of morals and of values that we have been presenting.

In brief, the explanation is this: if the goodness or worth or value of anything is to be equated simply with its perfection or actuality—or rather with its actuality considered precisely with reference to that prior potentiality that is ordered to such an actuality or perfection—then it is not only possible, but upon occasion might even be legitimate, to consider the qualities or properties of an object just as such and without reference to the fact of their being ordered to a prior state or condition, as actualities are to potentialities.[7] To employ an analogy, may not one consider the

---

Particularly it must not be thought that, as regards the specific examples which we are employing (of Mrs. Bennet or of Socrates), we are implying that Hume would necessarily disagree with our judgments of such cases in view of the inadequacies of his general ethical position. To the contrary, it is conceivable that Hume might be the first to recognize the folly of Mrs. Bennet or the nobility of Socrates. Yet if he were to do so, he would have to explain his judgments as being prompted not by the facts of the case, but simply by such attitudes of approval or disapproval as the facts might happen to have evoked in him. In other words, it is only this latter notion of Hume's as to the grounds of his moral judgments that we are criticizing, and not at all the actual moral judgments themselves that he either did make or might conceivably have made.

7. Aquinas speaks directly to this point *The Disputed Questions on Truth*, Vol. III, trans. R. W. Schmidt (Chicago: Henry Regnery, 1954), pp. 4–5, 9. The objection is raised: "Whenever things are so related that one adds something to the other either really or conceptually, one can be understood without the other. But being cannot be understood without good. Hence good does not add anything to being either really or conceptually" (Qu. 23, Art. 1, To the Contrary 2'). St. Thomas' response is: "To this it must be said that a thing can be understood without another in two ways. (1) This occurs by way of enunciating, when one thing is understood *to be* without

properties of smoke, say, without any reference to the fact that they are effects of fire? Yet merely because it is thus possible to consider smoke simply in itself, and apart from any and every connection that it may have with fire, that certainly does not mean that it has no such real connection, or that this connection may not be readily recognized the minute one considers smoke not just as it is in itself and in abstraction from such relationships as it may enter into, but rather concretely and in the connections and contexts that it has as a matter of fact and in its real existence.

Such an analogy between potency-act and cause-effect might seem at first to render our hoped-for counterarguments against Hume more implausible than plausible. For it was Hume who built his reputation on a practice of taking common-sense examples of cause-effect and showing that repeated experience with such causes never sufficed to disclose any necessary connection between cause and effect. Accordingly, just as our ability to consider effects in abstraction from any relation they might have to their causes was one of the decisive grounds for Hume's insistence that we have no basis for supposing that there is any necessary connection between cause and effect at all, so also one might argue that our ability to consider the actual properties of an object in abstraction from the relation they bear to prior potentialities of that same object must be taken to mean that there is no sort of necessary relation or connection of act to potency or of potency to act.

Now clearly this is not the place to mount a full-scale refutation of Hume's skepticism regarding the necessary connections between cause and effect. It may be sufficient merely to remark on the comparative irrelevance—to say nothing of the farfetched character—of Hume's skepticism in the present connection. For supposing that there were some sort

---

the other. Whatever the intellect can understand without another in this sense, God can make without the other. But being cannot be so understood without good, i.e. so that the intellect understands that something is a being and is not good. (2) Something can be understood without another by way of defining, so that the intellect understands one without at the same time understanding the other. Thus animal is understood without man or any of the other species. In this sense being can be understood without good. Yet it does not follow that God can make a being without good, because the very notion of making is to bring into existence" (Answers to Contrary Difficulties 2).

of a necessary connection between cause and effect,[8] there certainly would be no reason to suppose that one could not consider the particular features and characteristics that a given effect might have just in itself and quite apart from any concern with how such features might involve a dependence on a cause. In other words, the mere fact that an effect may be considered in abstraction from its cause by no means implies that such an effect is not in fact necessarily dependent upon a cause, or that such a dependence may not be recognizable and intelligible once we turn our attention from a consideration of the properties of the effect just as such to a consideration of the effect precisely in its relations of dependence upon a cause.

What is directly relevant to the ontology of morals and ethics is not the cause-effect relation, but rather the relation of potency to act. Hence, whteher this relation is analogous to that of cause-effect or not, there is surely nothing in the very nature and character of the potency-act relation that would either (1) preclude our being able to consider the actual features of an object in abstraction from their relation to a prior state of potentiality in that object, or (2) would entail any denial of the very possibility of such a relationship, the minute it was suposed that the one term of the relation might be able to be considered in abstraction from the other.

Returning to Hume's celebrated contention that virtue and vice are not matters of fact, we have but to emend his wording slightly and then to continue on in a somewhat different vein, in order to see just how and why his contention should have so plausible a ring to it while it is really quite arbitrary and ill-founded.

Take any action allowed to be vicious:
Willful murder, for instance. Examine it in a certain light, and of course you will not find that matter of fact, or real existence, which you call vice. Taking it in this way, you will find only certain passions, volitions and thoughts.
But this, of course, is not the only light in which willful murder may

---

8. This is a supposition which Hume would be the first to admit is perfectly conceivable. His problem is that although it is conceivable, he is unable to find any evidence either a priori or a a posteriori that it is in fact the case.

be examined, or even the fullest and brightest light. For 'tis only when the action of willful murder be taken in abstraction from its concrete and proper context as the action of a human being of definite potentialities and capabilities, and who by such an action did thus inhibit himself from developing into the sort of person and character that he could and should have been—only in the half-light of such abstraction doth it appear that an action of willful murder is wholly neutral, being neither vicious nor virtuous. Thus you have but to return this action to its proper context, and then its vice will not escape you even when you consider the object and the object alone. Rather 'tis only when you consider the object in the abstract, and apart from the necessary relationships into which it enters in its concrete existence, that the vice doth then seem to escape you.

And so by a bit of fanciful tailoring of Hume's very words, we can almost refute him out of his own mouth, the minute he begins in his accustomed vein to insist that virtue and vice are not matters of fact at all, and that from any examination of the object the virtue and the vice will entirely escape us. We can also see just how Hume could have become so blind to moral and ethical distinctions. For we can indeed look at an object in such a way that its virtue and vice will entirely escape us. And this is just what Hume did.

The explanation is not far to seek, given the particular ontological account of the nature and character of objects that we have here been putting forward. For the so-called properties of an object, in addition to being just what they are as such, are also actualities of prior potentialities in the object. Indeed, in this latter respect, they even have the character of "perfections" answering to that *appetitus* for completion and fulfillment that any potentiality simply is. Any particular property, *a,* in addition to being just itself, namely, *a,* is at the same time something desirable, when considered in its relation to the *appetitus* of a prior potentiality. But so also is it something intelligible when considered in relation to a possible knower or knowers.[9] And no less is it an effect when considered in relation to the causes that produced it. Accordingly, all of these further features of *a* that are, as it were, supervenient and characterize *a,* just

9. See the references that are given in Chapter VI above, nn. 17, 20.

insofar as it stands in relation to other things—to causes, to prior potentialities, to knowers, etc.—may, of course, be abstracted from *a* so that *a* may be considered just in itself.

Nevertheless, the mere fact that something may thus be considered in abstraction from certain of the features that pertain to it by no means implies that that thing can actually exist in abstraction from such supervenient aspects, or even that one can fail to see that the thing has these, the minute the thing is considered not in abstraction but in its concreteness. Right here, then, would appear to be the source of Hume's mistake and of his unfortunate blindness. For the mere fact that objective facts can be viewed in abstraction from the values and disvalues that pertain to them certainly does not mean either that they must be so viewed or that values and disvalues are not factual and objective.

An Ancient Brief Exhibit
of Empirical Method in Ethics

Hume's habits of value-blindness and moral blindness have been considerably reinforced since his time, largely by the fact that it has become the ingrained practice of scientists to view the objective facts of nature in complete abstraction from all those supervenient ontological relationships that such facts necessarily enter into. Yet why, in our efforts to know and understand the real world in which we human beings find ourselves, must we necessarily be guided by the practice of modern scientists? For it is by no means clear that the primary purpose of science is to achieve a knowledge of reality at all; and certainly its purpose is not to achieve a knowledge of the real in its concreteness and fullness.

Indeed, in order that we might have just a taste of what the possibilities of human knowledge are, once we have liberated ourselves from the accustomed scientific restrictions of value-blindness, we might allow ourselves a brief lapse from meta-ethics into ethics, not for the purpose of demonstrating any actual ethical conclusions, but simply to illustrate the possibilities and resources for an open and unrestricted empirical approach to matters of ethics. Just consider how Aristotle proposes no less than a straightforward rational consideration of the facts of human experience as the means that he would adopt for finding answers to the basic questions of ethics.[10]

We may now return to the Good which is the object of our search, and try to find out exactly what it can be. For good appears to be one thing in one pursuit or art and another in another; it is different in medicine from what it is in strategy, and so with the rest of the arts. What definition of the Good then will hold true in all the arts? Perhaps we may define it as that for the sake of which everything else is done. This applies to something different in each different art—to health in the case of medicine, to victory in that of strategy, to a house in architecture and to something else in each of the other arts: But in every pursuit or undertaking it describes the end of that pursuit or undertaking, since in all of them it is for the sake of the end that everything else is done. Hence if there be something which is the end of all things done by human action, this will be the practicable Good—or if there be several such ends, the sum of these will be the Good. . . .

Perhaps then we may arrive at this by ascertaining what is man's function. For the goodness or efficiency of a fluteplayer or sculptor or craftsman of any sort, and in general of anybody who has some function or business to perform, is thought to reside in that function; and similarly it may be held that the good of man resides in the function of man, if he has a function.

Are we then to suppose that, while the carpenter and the shoemaker have definite functions or businesses belonging to them, man as such has none, and is not designed by nature to fulfill any function? Must we not rather assume that just as the eye, the hand, the foot and each of the various members of the body manifestly has a certain function of its own, so a human being also has a certain function over and above all the functions of his particular members? What then precisely can this function be? The mere act of living appears to be shared even by plants, whereas we are looking for the function peculiar to man; we must therefore set aside the vital activity of nutrition and growth. Next in the scale will come some form of sentient life; but this too appears to be shared by horses, oxen, and animals generally. There remains therefore what may be called the practical life of man as possessing reason.[11]

10. For a most impressive contemporary attempt at doing much the same thing, see Mortimer Adler, *The Time of Our Lives* (New York: Holt, Rinehart and Winston, 1970).

11. Aristotle *Nicomachean Ethics,* 2d ed., trans. H. Rackham, Loeb Classical Library (New York, 1934), pp. 1097a15–25, 1097b24–1098a4; last line slightly altered.

In short, we have only to reread these familiar passages and it is at once borne in upon us how for Aristotle it presents no serious epistemological problem at all that we should be able to discern directly in experience the ends of things and the respective goods at which the various kinds of things aim. Specifically, Aristotle thinks he can determine what the good for man is simply by finding out what man's function (or *ergon*) is, and for him man's function is to be understood in terms of the nature of man and of the kind of being a human being is. Moreover, once we know not only what a thing is (i.e., what kind of a thing it is and what its nature is) but also what its proper function or mode of life or even more generally its proper mode of being is, then it becomes in principle a comparatively easy matter to determine whether in a given case a particular individual either measures up or falls short of what such a thing might be or could be in virtue of its nature and of the kind of thing that it is.[12] That is why in the case of someone like Mrs. Bennet it becomes possible for us to recognize her shortcomings just as a human being; and likewise, by way of contrast, it is equally possible for us to appreciate the virtues and achievements of a man like Socrates—we have only to see them or consider them in the light of the standard of human nature itself. Moreover, the materials from which we may thus derive such knowledge of the wise and the unwise, of the noble and the petty, in human existence are supplied to us not from the sciences, in the modern sense of that term, but directly from our own everyday human experience, as well as from art, from literature, from history, and from the humanities generally.

If at first we feel a bit put off by the odd and perhaps even dubious-sounding phrase "the standard of human nature," which is the sort of thing that must serve as our standard in the pursuit of such humanistic learning as is relevant to ethics, we have only to consider that it is not just man's nature or human nature that can function as a standard, but

12. This should not be taken to mean that such a knowledge may not be extremely difficult to attain, being as it is highly fallible and constantly corrigible. In fact, in this brief sketch we make no pretense at having solved the epistemological problems which the conception of such a knowledge gives rise to. Rather we would hope only to have given some indication of what the logic of this type of knowledge must be. On this whole issue, see Veatch, *Two Logics.*

the natures of things generally.[13] A cat, a tree, a rosebush, a fish—indeed, everything of whatever kind may be a more or less good specimen of its kind. We all know perfectly well that cats can be mangy, trees stunted in their growth, rosebushes sickly from being eaten up by bugs, and fish half-starved from lack of food. Moreover, in all such cases we never doubt for a minute but that our judgments are of such a kind as to be altogether objective and factually grounded: the cat really is sick, the rosebush is hardly what a rosebush might be or could be, the poor fish is just that, "a poor fish!" And in each such case, our judgments are based on a regard for what the thing is that we are considering, i.e., the kind of thing it is as well as what its proper or characteristic function (*ergon*) or activity is. In short, since a thing can hardly be other than the kind of thing it is, its very nature or "what" or quiddity is no less than a built-in, objective standard in terms of which that particular thing's shortcomings or, as the case may be, its "full-comings" may be objectively judged and determined.

And so it is with respect to human beings—we come to recognize what man is, what his nature or quiddity is, and with that we can also see what his function is, what the standard is, in other words, of a man's being truly human. What is that standard in the case of man? It is simply that of being a rational animal. This, indeed, is the very heart and core of a natural-law ethic.

Ethics without Ontology:

Its Implication for Utilitarianism

In the title of this chapter, the term "epistemology of morals" was used. Is the reader, then, to suppose that the section immediately preceding made pretense of actually providing such an epistemology? Of course not. For present purposes it is sufficient for us merely to have indicated not how such an epistemology is to be developed out of an ontology of

13. See Aquinas' remarks to the effect that there will be a diversity of natural laws and a diversity of goods according to the diversity of natural kinds, *Summa Theologiae* I–II. 91. 6.

morals but merely how in principle it might be so developed, and what the logic of such a development might be.

Nevertheless, having thus started a number of epistemological hares, it might be instructive if in this last chapter we were to go behind the two dominant movements in contemporary ethical theory, existentialism and linguistic analysis, and consider their two principal forerunners, utilitarianism and so-called Kantian or deontological ethics. What is interesting about these two earlier movements is that they both represent attempts at providing an epistemological grounding for ethics, not merely in the complete absence of anything like an ontology of act and potency but of any ontology of morals at all. Hence we might do well to examine these earlier efforts to bring off an epistemology of ethics without an ontology, just to see how successful they were. Moreover, since much of contemporary ethical theory is shot through with both utilitarianism and Kantianism, it will be interesting to notice how it is just this background of an attempted ethics without ontology that has made it almost inevitable that contemporary moral philosophers should sooner or later have resorted to the transcendental turn.

Needless to say, in labeling these two traditions the "utilitarian" and the "Kantian," we are using such terms broadly, not to say loosely. Indeed it might be less misleading, even if less familiar, if our terminology were designed simply to point a contrast between a "desire-ethic" and a "duty-ethic." But, however one may label them, it can hardly be denied that two quite different trends or traditions in modern ethical theory are discernible, and that both are alike in being projects of an ethics without ontology. Accordingly, we shall for the most part refer to the one tradition as a desire-ethic and the other as a duty-ethic.

First, then, let us have a look at the desire-ethic of utilitarianism. Surely, in most if not all varieties of utilitarianism, it is commonly held that the source of moral and ethical distinctions, not to mention values as well, is to be located not in the object but in the subject. As Hume insisted, so long as you consider just the object, you will never find either values or moral or ethical distinctions there. It is only when you turn your reflection into your own breast, and there come across various feelings and sentiments toward or about such objects, that you discover what the sources are of things or objects being good or bad, or of actions being right or wrong. That is to say, they are not good or bad, or right or wrong, in themselves; they are so only in virtue of how we feel about them—whether we like or dislike them, approve or disapprove of them, whether they give us pleasure or pain, etc. Nor does it really make any difference whether value is thought of as attaching to or being in the object as a result of the latter's being liked or desired, or whether, in accordance with the hedonism of most of the classical utilitarians, value is equated simply with that pleasure which arises in us—in the subject— when a desired object is attained and that particular desire is thus satisfied. The important thing is that the value or worth of an object is reckoned as having no ontological status in the object just as such, but rather as being entirely a function of the subject's desire or liking for the object.[14]

Moreover, as soon as values are thus denied an objective ontological status, then certain epistemological consequences would seem to follow. For one thing, to learn what things are good or bad, or what actions are right or wrong, one may no longer look to those things or actions themselves; rather, as Hume says, one must turn one's reflection into one's own breast to see how one feels about such things and actions. Or, to put it a little differently, if as human beings we want to know how to act, or what the right life for a human being is, it is of no use to give ourselves over to the study of the humanities and to make of man the proper study of mankind, as though from coming to know what man is we

14. Perhaps one possible misunderstanding needs to be guarded against here. No doubt most moral philosophers of the present day, influenced as they almost inevitably are by Moore's notion of naturalism in ethics and of the naturalistic fallacy, would tend to suppose that a desire-ethic could hardly be other than an example of ethical naturalism. But any ethical naturalism must certainly be said to have ontological import. For is it not the point of the naturalistic fallacy that value properties and moral properties are mistakenly identified with certain natural or real properties of things? How, then, can we suppose that a desire-ethic, so far from being ontologically grounded, really represents an attempt at ethics without ontology? We would hope that the foregoing paragraph in the text may have provided a sufficient answer to this question. We are using the expression "ontology of morals or ethics" to signify just that type of ethical theory which seeks to locate ethical and value distinctions in the facts, independently of their being desired, and not as a mere function of their being desired. From this standpoint, Moore's conception of ethical naturalism can only be somewhat misleading.

might thereby get some idea of what he ought to be. Far from it, for quite apart from any supposed logical difficulties connected with the naturalistic fallacy or with trying to derive an "ought" from an "is," from the standpoint of a desire-ethic it is simply irrelevant and beside the point for anyone ever to try to learn about the worth or value of anything by considering what such a thing is objectively. Once more, it is not what a thing is objectively that determines its goodness, but how we feel about it. As for these feelings and desires that we have toward objects, it is not because a thing is good that we desire it or have the pro-attitude toward it that we do, but rather it is because we desire it that we call it good.

Right here, though, it would seem that a serious difficulty arises that must necessarily beset any desire-ethic so conceived and so understood. For how can it even claim to be so much as an ethics at all? We have already noted that apparently the hallmark of any properly moral or ethical judgment is that it must be a reasoned judgment.[15] That is to say, it must be a judgment to which reasons are in principle relevant, even though the person making the judgment may not have thought much about such reasons or even be able to produce any such on demand. In contrast, what about judgments that express our desires and likings? Apparently, many if not most of these are judgments for which reasons would seem to be hardly relevant. Thus, recalling our earlier example, if I say that I like spinach and I am asked "Why?" I may quite properly say that I don't know why, I just do, that's all. And the point is that when it comes to mere likes and desires, reasons are not relevant to these at all, but only causes.

Perhaps, though, it might be well if we sought to pose this difficulty rather more directly in terms of principles and considerations that are particularly current and fashionable among contemporary ethical theo-rists. Thus the one thing that is constantly stressed in the recent literature is what is sometimes called the *universalizability* of moral and ethical judgments. Hare, for example, gives almost dogmatic pronouncement to the simple fact of such universalizability: "If you call X a good Y, you are committed to the judgment that anything which is like X in the

15. See Chapter II above, esp. pp. 27–32.

relevant respects is also a good Y." [16] Giving expression to a somewhat different facet of this same universalizability, Marcus Singer enunciates what he calls the generalization principle, "that what is right (or wrong) for one person must be right (or wrong) for any similar person in similar circumstances." [17]

As to just why such universalizability should attach to moral judgments and value judgments—whether it is simply a fact of logic or of language or of nature—we shall not take time to consider. Let us accept it as simply a fact. Admitting it to be a fact, the problem then becomes one of trying to figure out how such judgments as are made in the context of a desire-ethic can ever be susceptible of such universalizability or generalization. Thus if my calling X a good Y is but the consequence of my finding it to be a Y that I like or that gives me pleasure or that I want, then it would hardly seem that such a judgment would be universalizable in the requisite sense. For it simply is not true that in calling X a good Y for no other reason than that it is a Y which I like or fancy, I am thereby committed to finding anything that is like X in the relevant respects to be a Y that I like or fancy equally well. After all, one's desires and likings are notoriously whimsical: what pleases me at one time may very well repel me or leave me quite indifferent the next time.[18] And *mutatis mutandis,* of course, what holds with respect to Hare's example would seem to be no less applicable to Singer's generaliza-

---

16. R. M. Hare, *Freedom and Reason* (New York: Oxford University Press, Galaxy Books, 1965), p. 18.

17. Marcus Singer, *Generalization in Ethics* (New York: Alfred A. Knopf, 1961), p. 5.

18. Of course, this is not to say that likes and dislikes might not be subsumed under universal psychological laws, in which case my liking X, for example, might be taken to imply that anyone like me, with my peculiar traits and situated in like circumstances, would like X as well. However, such a psychological universalizability, if we may so term it, is a very different affair from the universalizability of goodness, such as recent thinkers like Hare and others have been wont to press. For, as we have already noted in earlier chapters, a predicate like "good" or "right" not only is universalizable, but also carries with it the further implication that there are reasons for such goodness or rightness. In contrast, while predicates such as "liked," "desired," "pleasant," etc., may upon occasion be universalizable, they are nevertheless predicates of a kind to which causes are relevant rather than reasons. This, however, is a point which we shall have more to say about in the immediate sequel.

tion principle. For if the fact that a certain course of action is considered right for someone betokens no more than that someone finds such a course to be pleasing or to his liking, then it hardly follows that it would be found equally pleasing or to his liking if performed by another, though similar, person in similar circumstances.[19]

Apparently, then, there is a serious difficulty here: either universalizability is not a necessary feature of the logical grammar of ethical terms, or else such judgments as are made in the context of desire-ethics are not and cannot be ethical judgments at all.

Consider, too, that further characteristic of moral and ethical judgments which, no less than universalizability, is another thing that contemporary ethical theorists, particularly among the linguistic analysts, are ever given to harping upon. This is the feature of such judgments being reasoned judgments. Indeed, this susceptibility of ethical judgments to being reasoned judgments is inseparable from their universalizability. Thus suppose, for instance, that you were to come across an American—presumably of a bygone era—who claimed that as a matter of right he was entitled to life, liberty, and the pursuit of happiness. How might he justify such a claim? Clearly, the very logic of the example requires that any such particular claim be justified by showing it to be a particular case falling under a more general rule. Accordingly, our American might claim the right to life, liberty, and the pursuit of happiness for himself simply on the ground that he is a man, and that such rights are the inalienable rights of any and every human being.

So it is that the possibility of giving reasons for moral judgments and the universalizability of such judgments go together. As Singer remarks:

> The generalization principle . . . is involved in or presupposed by every genuine moral judgment, for it is an essential part of the meaning of such distinctively moral terms as "right," "wrong," and "ought," in

---

19. Singer would doubtless object that such a consideration is quite irrelevant, that the generalization principle is binding upon me, regardless of whether an action which I recommend for myself proves equally attractive to me when it is recommended for someone else. The answer is that the generalization principle cannot thus become binding upon me until my own original recommendation to myself is couched in ethical terms rather than in mere terms of liking or attractiveness; and that is just the issue!

their distinctively moral senses. It is also an essential feature of moral reasoning, for it is presupposed in every attempt to give a reason for a moral judgment. It thus determines what can count as a moral reason. . . .

It follows from this that there can be no genuine moral judgment apart from reasons, and no moral reasons apart from the generalization principle.[20]

Apparently Singer's pronouncements on this score are decisive and definitive. Yet must they not at the same time play havoc with any desire-ethic, whether of the strict utilitarian variety, or even of Singer's own variety? For, as we have seen, the basic anti-ontological thesis of such an ethic necessitates that the goodness of anything be regarded as a function of its being desired. Yet are not desires and likings often responses, on the part of ourselves as subjects, for which no reasons can be given but only causes? Indeed, if a desire or a liking or an interest or a preference or what not should ever be such that a reason could be given for it, then that reason would have to consist ultimately in some sort of appeal to the worth or excellence or goodness of that which was being desired or liked or preferred. This, however, would be tantamount to saying that in such a case the object of desire was desired because it was good, rather than being good because it was desired—and this would be to go counter to the very first principle of any desire-ethic. What, then, does this leave as the only alternative open to a desire-ethic? It is the alternative of having to say that ultimately and in the last analysis our desires must be unreasoned. But if the goodness of things—and the same would hold for all other ethical or value predicates as well—were no more than a function of their being desired, then it would be no more possible to give reasons for judging something to be good than it would be for judging it to be liked or desired. And this last would seem to go counter to what everyone seems to think is an essential feature of any and every moral or ethical judgment.

Thus, just on the face of it, any sort of desire-ethic would appear to be in a dilemma: either it must sacrifice its fundamental, anti-ontological first principle that constitutes it a desire-ethic in the first place; or it must

20. Singer, *Generalization in Ethics*, p. 34; see also p. 24.

admit to not being an ethics at all, there being no way in which, in the context of such a supposed ethics, any ethical judgments could possibly be made.

Ethics without Ontology:
Its Implications for Kantian Ethics

Let us have a look at that other major tradition in modern ethics, which derives its inspiration largely from Kant, and which we have chosen to label a duty-ethic, or a deontological ethics. Once again, we predict that an examination of this type of ethical theory will show it to be up against a dilemma, no less than were the utilitarians, albeit a dilemma of a rather different sort.

Whereas for the utilitarians one horn of the dilemma was that ethical distinctions seemed hardly applicable to mere desires, likings, inclinations, etc., for the partisans of a duty-ethic this is no problem or, perhaps we should say, no horn at all. Instead, it is a fundamental conviction of Kant's that such things as desires, inclinations, and so on are, if not downright irrelevant to ethics, then at least ethically or morally neutral. There is no way, as Kant sees it, for desires and inclinations to remain such and yet come to acquire or become invested with some sort of moral quality or other. For that matter, the very arguments that we advanced against a desire-ethic, to the effect that desires are neither universalizable nor susceptible of rational justification, are really Kantian in their inspiration.

For Kant, desires and inclinations are just the sorts of things for which no reasons but only causes can be given. Hence to appeal to any sort of inclination or natural tendency as being the basis or ground for our actions would be to accede, as Kant would say, to a mere *heteronomy* of the will rather than an *autonomy*. In the *Groundwork*,[21] Kant says:

> Wherever an object of the will has to be put down as the basis for prescribing a rule to determine the will, there the rule is heteronomy; the

21. Immanuel Kant, *Groundwork of the Metaphysic of Morals,* trans. H. J. Paton (New York: Harper and Row, Torchbooks, 1964), pp. 93-95.

imperative is conditioned as follows: "*If,* or *because,* you will this object, you ought consequently to act thus or thus." . . . However, the object determines the will [22]—whether by means of inclination, as in the principle of personal happiness, or by means of reasons directed to objects of our possible volitions generally, as in the principle of perfection—the will never determines itself immediately by the thought of an action, but only by the impulsion which the anticipated effect of the action exercises on the will: "*I ought to do something because I will something else.*" And the basis for this must be yet a further law in me as a subject, whereby I necessarily will this "something else." . . . The impulsion supposed to be exercised on the will of the subject, in accordance with his natural constitution, by the idea of a result to be attained by his own powers belongs to the nature of the subject—whether to his sensibility (his inclinations and taste) or to his understanding and reason, whose operation on an object is accompanied by satisfaction in virtue of the special equipment of their nature—and consequently, strictly speaking, it is nature which would make the law. This law as a law of nature . . . is *always merely heteronomy of the will:* the will does not give itself the law, but an alien impulsion does so through the medium of the subject's own nature as tuned for its reception.

In other words, if desire is the basis of an action, then that action cannot in any sense be moral, simply for the reason that to act from desire or inclination cannot ultimately be anything but an unreasoned action, caused simply by "an alien impulsion." "In that case the subject would attribute the determination of his power of judgment not to his reason, but to an impulsion." [23]

Moreover, just as Kant might be interpreted as faulting any desire-ethic on the ground that all desires are ultimately unreasoned and hence radically non-ethical or extra-ethical, so likewise it would seem that judgments as to what one may do, based on what one is inclined to do or wants to do, are equally non-moral, simply because they are not universalizable. That is why Kant will not hear of any appeal to human nature as a basis for judgments as to what we ought to do or how we ought to act:

22. Clearly, Kant here thinks of an object as determining the will not because it is thought to be good or worthwhile in itself, but simply in the manner of a cause rather than that of a reason.

23. Kant, *Groundwork,* p. 101.

The universality with which these laws should hold for all rational beings without exception . . . falls away if their basis is taken from the *special constitution of human nature* or from the accidental circumstances in which it is placed.[24]

We should not dream for a moment of trying to derive the reality of this principle from *the special characteristics of human nature*. For duty has to be a practical, unconditioned necessity of action; it must therefore hold for all rational beings (to whom alone an imperative can apply at all), and *only because of this* can it also be a law for all human wills. Whatever, on the other hand, is derived from the special predisposition of humanity, from certain feelings and propensities, and even, if this were possible, from some special bent peculiar to human reason and not holding necessarily for the will of every rational being—all this can indeed supply a personal maxim, but not a law: it can give us a subjective principle—one on which we have a propensity and inclination to act— but not an objective one on which we should be *directed* to act although our every propensity, inclination and natural bent were opposed to it.[25]

Very well, then, since desires are neither open to rational justification nor susceptible of generalization or universalizability, they cannot possibly be the sources of our moral judgments and evaluation—at least not as Kant sees the picture. Does that mean, then, that Kant accepts what we have called an ontological basis for ethics as the only alternative to a desire-ethic? After all, as we have seen, a desire-ethic may perhaps best be construed as little more than a reaction against what might be called the objectivism of an ontologically-based ethics. Recall once more Hume's celebrated counsel: if moral distinctions are never to be found so long as you direct your attention to the object, the thing to do is to turn your reflection into your own breast and there you will find feelings, sentiments, desires, etc., which are the sources of the moral distinctions and evaluations that we come to invest objects with. Accordingly, if Kant consistently denies that feelings and desires can ever be the proper and legitimate sources of morality, does that mean that he would have us return once again to the objects, from which Hume had directed our

24. *Ibid.*, p. 90.
25. *Ibid.*, pp. 59–60.

attention away? Of course, the answer is "No." For a duty-ethic of the Kantian type is no less anti-ontological than is a desire-ethic of the utilitarian type. Yet right here in its repudiation of ontology are the sources of serious difficulties for Kantian ethics, to say nothing of a dilemma as embarrassing as that confronting a desire-ethic.

Where, in fact, is Kant to turn in order to ground his ethics, if the source of such duties and obligations as are incumbent upon us is to be found neither in us, in our feelings, inclinations, desires, etc., nor in the nature of objects as they are independently of how we may feel about them? Clearly, Kant cannot proceed in the manner of the natural-law moralists, trying to determine what man is objectively, what his natural end is, and what those natural laws are that man must observe if he is to attain that perfection toward which just as a human being he is naturally ordered. To proceed in such wise as a means of coming to know what we ought to do and be would, in Kant's eyes, be to commit ourselves to heteronomy. Any natural end or natural perfection of anything, Kant would say, is something to the pursuit of which we must be causally determined; and therefore it is not anything to which we can determine ourselves rationally, or for which we can give any reasons. For that matter, let any object or any end whatever determine the will, and then, Kant insists, there will be a situation in which "the will does not give itself the law, but the object does so in virtue of its relation to the will." [26]

In one sense Kant is right in all this. If an end, whether natural or otherwise, does determine us in such a way that we find ourselves naturally inclining or tending toward it, but we cannot say why (i.e., "why" in the sense of giving a reason, as contrasted with merely giving a cause for such a tendency or inclination)—then any such tendency or inclination is not morally significant. But what Kant fails to realize is that, in addition to desiring or tending toward certain ends for no reason, we can desire or tend toward something because we recognize it as being good or worthwhile. To paraphrase our old formula once again, not only do we call things good because they are desired, but in addition we can and often do desire things simply because we recognize them to be good. Thus from the standpoint of a natural-law ethic, the mere fact that

26. *Ibid.*, p. 88.

an end is natural—that it is the actuality or perfection of a corresponding potentiality—does not preclude it from being good. Moreover, given a rational being, as we may assume that a human being is, it is possible for him to come to recognize the goodness or intrinsic excellence of that way of life toward which he is naturally oriented; and having thus recognized the goodness of his natural end, he can pursue it, not from being naturally determined or moved thereto, but rather from being rationally determined thereto in that he sees that it is good and thus comes to desire and seek it for that reason. Now Kant, as we say, seems strangely blind to even the possibility of this latter alternative.[27]

Consider, though, just what this blindness means and what insuperable difficulties it creates for a duty-ethic type of theory. For if the objective study of nature, particularly of human nature, cannot give us even an inkling as to what is required of us ethically or morally, how else and from what other source can we possibly acquire such knowledge? Clearly, Kant's prohibitions—and seemingly quite justifiable prohibitions—will not allow us to follow the way of Hume and of the utilitarians to try to find the sources of ethics in our human reactions to objects in terms of feelings and desires. But then where can we go, if neither within our own breasts nor outside are we able to find any evidence of the ethical?

As is well known, Kant appeals to what he calls "practical reason" as being the proper source of our moral and ethical knowledge. But with that, the floodgates are opened to those murky Kantian waters, filled with strange doctrines of the intelligible world as over against the phenomenal world, and of how and why it is that only practical reason and not theoretical reason is competent to provide any kind of knowledge of the former. Perhaps we can simply pass over these in silence, for the relevant

---

27. Perhaps this is being unfair to Kant. It may be that he is not so much blind to the possibility of such an alternative as merely skeptical of all attempts that have thus far been made to flesh out this alternative in the concrete. For suppose that we admit the possibility of an objective goodness or perfection of human life and human existence; has anyone ever been able to state specifically what this consists in, without thereby compromising the autonomy of the will and condemning it to a mere heteronomy? Now does Kant really mean to imply no more than this in his apparent rejection of the alternative of a thing's being desired simply because it is good, rather than good because it is desired? Unhappily, we simply do not understand Kant's ethics well enough to be able to answer this question.

consideration for our purposes is simply that, whether it is called practical or theoretical, it is a kind of knowledge that Kant claims to have, so far as the basic principles of ethics are concerned. But again, just where does this knowledge come from, and just what is it that we must look at and investigate in order to gain such a knowledge of ethical principles? To investigate human nature will do no good, for the reasons we have already considered. Perhaps, though, if it is not from a consideration of "the special constitution of human nature" that we find out what sorts of duties and obligations are incumbent upon us, then maybe it is from a consideration of the nature of rational beings just as such.

Even this will not do. If Kant appeals merely from the nature of men to that of rational beings generally in order to determine what the moral laws are, then his method would be one of seeking an ontological basis for his ethics after all. The only thing to distinguish his ethical theory from that of a natural-law ethics of the traditional sort would be that Kant was substituting the nature of rational beings in general (as offering the ultimate basis for his natural moral laws) for the nature of man. And this would be heteronomy all over again, albeit at one higher remove in the generic scale.

So long as Kant is either unwilling or unable to recognize the possibility that a natural desire may nonetheless be a reasoned desire and thus determined by nothing less than a knowledge of the good, he must renounce altogether any and all attempts to provide an ontological basis for ethics in terms of a thing's nature, be it human nature or the nature of rational beings generally. But the question returns to plague the Kantians more persistently than ever: how can one possibly come to know the moral laws that are incumbent upon us as rational beings if appeal is not to be made to the nature of such beings by way of support? So far as we have been able to determine, the only way that a Kantian can answer this question is by attempting to appeal not to the nature of rational beings, but rather to the purely formal requirements that presumably must attach to moral laws, insofar as these laws are held to be binding on all rational creatures. One might then say that although he did not know what particular moral laws were thus binding upon rational beings, at least he would know that such laws must have the form of principles that are at once reasoned and universalizable.

Unfortunately, it is hard to see how one could ever know that such moral laws as were binding upon rational creatures must have these purely formal features, unless one recognized that laws of this form were required by the very nature of rational beings—and in this sense the formal features of one's ethics, no less than its material features, would be determined in the light of the particular ontological basis that one gives to one's ethics. One even wonders if it might be along just such lines as these that Kant himself might try to justify his contention that moral laws must have the particular formal features that he ascribes to them. For why might not Kant appeal simply to the nature of a moral being as at once rational and free? Would this not provide him with a basis for his contention that moral laws must have the formal properties of being at least reasoned and universalizable, i.e., of being categorical imperatives? It is doubtful, though, that Kant ever does anything of quite this sort. Indeed, had he done so, then his purely formalistic ethic might have acquired a much-needed support and justification, although at the price of a certain inconsistency.

Still, whatever may be true of Kant, it would seem that, at least among the present-day linguistic analysts who have tried to adapt certain features of Kantian ethics to their own purposes, the effort has been made to recognize the purely formal features of moral laws, without attempting to explain and account for such features in terms of the peculiar nature and constitution of rational, moral beings. Rather, it is asserted, supposedly on no more than linguistic or logical grounds, that moral principles must have such and such a formal character, or that the logical grammar of moral and ethical terms manifests certain recognizable formal features. As to the success of these efforts to account for the formal features of moral judgments and moral reasoning simply in terms of logic and language and without any appeal to ontology at all, we shall have more to say later.

For the present, though, this is not what we wish to point up as being the most serious weakness of Kantian ethics. Rather its weakness lies precisely in its very formalism—a formalism which turns out to be as hopeless as it is ineradicable. From the standpoint of ethics, what good is it to know that such moral laws and moral principles as may be binding upon us must have certain formal characteristics, when we never can know, either in fact or in principle, what any of these laws are? Kant seems to believe that a knowledge of the formal requirements of moral laws is of value in that at least it is able to function negatively. That is to say, we can use these formal requirements as a touchstone for exhibiting how certain laws that men may put forward as being proper moral laws can be shown not to meet the test. Yet one is still inclined to ask what good it does to know only that certain supposed moral laws are not binding upon us, if we do not know what laws are thus binding. Nor would there appear to be any way in which specificity and content might be given to morals and ethics, unless some way were found in which we could determine what is morally incumbent upon us simply in virtue of our nature as men or as rational beings. For Kant, however, there is no way of determining this, simply because, having totally misconceived what an ontological basis for an ethics might be, he denies the very possibility of such a thing and so shuts off the one means open to him of introducing concreteness and specificity into his ethics. His dilemma, in short, is simply this: either he must recognize the possibility of an ontology of morals, thereby betraying what is perhaps the most fundamental principle of his own ethical theory; or he must simply acknowledge that his ethics ends in a formalism such that at best we can only know how to expose various proposed moral laws as being bogus, but without ever being able to know any specific moral laws to be sound.

A New Development in Ethics without Ontology,
at once Post-Kantian and Post-Utilitarian

Enough, then, by way of an initial critical assessment of these two dominant and almost antithetical tendencies in modern ethics and ethical theory. Of late, though, a rather odd thing seems to have been happening: it is as if the two tendencies had merged![28] Not that utilitarians have simply become Kantians, or Kantians utilitarians—hardly that! Yet, given the two dilemmas with which the two movements were respectively faced, it would appear that quite a number of contemporary ethical

---

28. One might say that Hare's book, *Freedom and Reason,* is one long, sustained effort to effect just such a merger.

theorists have chosen to seize one of the horns from each of the dilemmas, in the somewhat jaunty expectation that this might somehow leave no dilemma at all. Briefly, the tactic has been to simply take over the Kantian panoply of formal properties and formal requirements that attach to basic moral and ethical notions, and then to foist these upon a desire-ethic, as if the latter somehow offered a receptive material for the former. One might suspect that the result would be no more of a union than that of Siamese twins, but that remains to be seen.

In any case, the way the thing is supposed to work is this. The partisans of a desire-ethic have always insisted that our manifold human desires, interests, impulses, liking, etc., are alone proper materials for building a moral philosophy. If you and I and the next man all want to live our lives most fruitfully and in the best way possible, why worry about objective values and natural laws, supposedly inscribed in the very nature of things, or even about categorical imperatives and disinterested duties? Simply let each man consult his own interests, each going his own way, you doing what you want and I doing what I want, and, upon occasion, all of us doing what we collectively want.

Surely, this sounds most persuasive and attractive. Indeed, it is directly along these lines that the old tradition of a desire-ethic is supposed to be able to make its contributions to the new ethics. Yet no sooner is the contribution made than an odd and far-reaching consequence suddenly emerges—a consequence which traditional hedonists, utilitarians, interest-theorists, and others seem not always to have been too clearly aware of. For no sooner do I or do you begin to articulate our respective desire-ethics, I saying that it is all right for me to do what I want and to live my life as I please, and you saying that it is all right for you to do so, than suddenly both of us will be brought up sharp by the purely formal implications of a moral notion like "all right." In fact, something like Singer's generalization principle immediately comes into play, and seems almost to take over: what is right for one person must be right for any similar person in similar circumstances. So in my blissful and perhaps insouciant pursuit of my own interests and you of yours, we both find ourselves abruptly and quite unexpectedly confronted with unequivocal and inescapable moral obligations. If I consider that I have a right to do as I please, then I am bound (logically bound) to acknowledge that you have the same right; moreover, duties being correlative with rights, I must recognize that I have an actual duty to respect your rights, just as you do to respect mine; for that matter, you and I both have a duty to respect similar rights in all other men, just as they do to respect ours. In short, the domain of morality is suddenly upon us, and all around us, and there is no escaping from it!

Fortunately, there is neither need nor occasion for us to trace out the further implications and ramifications of these purely formal aspects of our everyday moral notions and concepts. Suffice it only to say that in richness and variety these would appear to outrun anything that Kant ever thought of in connection with his somewhat impoverished conception of the categorical imperative, even in its threefold formulation. For example, Singer has written a rather long and impressive book showing how the generalization principle—"what is right (or wrong) for one person might be right (or wrong) for any similar person in similar circumstances"—can be used to generate a peculiarly powerful moral argument, the so-called generalization argument—"if everyone were to do X, the consequences would be disastrous (or undesirable); therefore no one ought to do X." [29] Fortified with this principle and this argument, Singer devotes the rest of his book to showing in somewhat laborious detail "how moral perplexities can rationally be resolved, and how moral disputes can rationally be settled." [30] In short, ethics turns out to be a genuinely rational discipline after all.

To cite one other example, R. M. Hare's book, *Freedom and Reason,* opens with a deep bow to human freedom, which the author promptly construes in Hare-like fashion to be a freedom simply to make one's own decisions. Such decisions are not of a kind that can ever properly be compelled in any strict sense, certainly not by public authorities or by neighbors and fellow men, not by reason or by the facts of the case, not even by the rules of good English usage!—which last is something of a concession coming from a linguistic analyst! Having made his bow to freedom on the first page of his book, Hare notes on page two that at

29. Singer, *Generalization in Ethics,* p. 61.
30. *Ibid.,* p. 6.

the same time "the answering of moral questions is, or ought to be, a rational activity"; and again that "the answering of moral questions is [not] a quite arbitrary business, like the choice of one postage stamp from the sheet rather than another." [31]

What is it that introduces this element of rational compulsion, this unavoidable recognition that morality is not a purely arbitrary business, into the picture of those free and unfettered personal decisions which Hare had just painted on the preceding page? The answer is that it is simply the logic of moral notions and expressions, the purely formal requirements of the language of morals, that brings about this countervailing of freedom by reason. [32] Moreover, the single most distinctive logical feature of such moral notions is just their universalizability. It is this, indeed, and really this alone, that ultimately accounts for the restrictions placed upon freedom by reason, at least insofar as such restrictions are legitimate.

Thus just suppose—to borrow one of Hare's own illustrations [33] and adapt it to our own purposes—that I am a Nazi and that I don't like Jews in my community. In fact, I want to see them all carried off to the gas chambers and exterminated. Now in analyzing a somewhat gruesome situation such as this, Hare would presumably not fault my initial hatred of my Jewish neighbors, or my desire to see them exterminated, as being in itself morally reprehensible. It is only after my morally neutral feeling of aversion toward the Jews of my acquaintance is turned into a moral judgment to the effect that these Jews *ought to be,* or deserve to be, exterminated that I am likely to get into serious moral trouble, which, as Hare interprets it, turns out to be a kind of logical trouble. For if I say that my Jewish neighbors ought to be exterminated, this, as a moral judgment, is strictly universalizable: it commits me to the much more all-embracing judgment that not just my neighbors, but anyone—any human being, no matter who or what he may be, and no matter how

---

31. See Hare, *Freedom and Reason,* p. 2.
32. Of course, Hare might not accede to its being exactly a countervailing influence.
33. See his discussion in pt. II, chap. 9 of *Freedom and Reason.*

near and dear he may be even to me, provided only that he have Jewish blood in his veins—deserves to be carted off and consigned to the gas chambers.

But now, Hare comments, could I—that is to say, would I ever be willing to—accept this universalized and much more sweeping judgment to which my original use of the word "ought" commits me? Suppose I put to myself the possibility of its being discovered that, quite unbeknown to me or to anyone else, I actually had Jewish blood myself. Would I then be willing to accept the consequences of my original moral judgment, even as it now applies to me? Hare thinks not, supposing I were to be really honest about the matter. If I were not thus willing to accept the consequences of my judgment, when universalized, then I must repudiate my original moral judgment as also being one that I cannot accept. And so, we see, reason can be brought to bear on our moral judgments and decisions after all: my original judgment to the effect that my Jewish neighbors ought to be exterminated is now one that I see I must reject in the light of reason.

Of course, it is always possible that the light of reason might not have quite the effect that Hare foresees or would wish for. It is just conceivable that I might confound the predictions and come right out and accept the consequences of my universalized judgment after all, and do so honestly and in spite of everything. Oh, but Hare says, that would mean that I would then be no better than a "fanatic."

Let us not for the moment pursue this latter bit of rather more elusive profundity on Hare's part. Instead, before we undertake any criticisms of this general type of new-found ethics, which we have already suggested is a kind of amalgam of the traditions of both a desire- and a duty-ethic, it might be well first to take brief stock of its apparent virtues and achievements. For one thing, it really does succeed in seizing one horn of each of those dilemmas, the one of utilitarianism and the other of Kantianism. So far as the utilitarian dilemma is concerned, the new view simply denies that a desire-ethic falls short of being a morals or ethics at all, by Kantian standards. Those very formal features which Kant found to pertain necessarily to moral laws, as well as other related formal features which later thinkers have uncovered, are now held to be capable of superimposition directly upon a desire-ethic. Thus to recall our own rather simple earlier example: so far as a desire-ethic is concerned, all I need do is to couch in moral terms, say, my desire to do as I please by merely claiming that it is all right for me to do so, and at once I find myself committed to recognizing that other men have an equal right to do as they please, and that I have a duty to respect their right, just as they have a duty to respect mine. So far as Kantian ethics is concerned, the horn of the dilemma that has been so resolutely seized is that of its supposed hopeless and inevitable formalism. Thus it is simply denied that an ethics of the Kantian type is never able to be any more than purely formal or even formalistic. On the contrary, it is just our human desires, interests, tendencies, inclinations, etc., that are ready at hand as the proper materials of our moral life. One has but to invest these desires with various moral judgments based upon them, and at once the formal implications of such moral notions will then have taken over the game, as it were, and we shall find ourselves caught up in an entire network of moral obligation and mutual responsibility.

Now is the consequence merely one of dissolving the dilemmas and thus seemingly of being able to reconcile Kant and the utilitarians? Remember that what was particularly noteworthy about both the utilitarian and the Kantian traditions in ethics, as contrasted with what one finds in a natural-law ethic, is that both apparently thought that they could dispense with any ontological basis for ethics: moral and ethical distinctions just are not and cannot be objective facts about the world. Nevertheless, as we saw, this repudiation of ontology tended to cause rather serious epistemological difficulties for both of these ethical theories. For if one cannot, from examining the facts of the case, ever hope to know what one ought to do about that case, or if from studying human nature one can never find out what true human perfection or the good life for man consists in, then how is one to come by a knowledge of such things along either Kantian or utilitarian lines? So far as the partisans of a desire-ethic are concerned, it was Kant who quite effectively pointed out that it won't do to fall back on our sentiments and feelings about things and actions, as if they might be the source of our moral judgments upon these same things and actions. For feelings, desires, sentiments, etc., are at once unreasoned and incapable of that very kind of universality which is essential to any properly moral judgment. And as for Kant himself, no less of an epistemological difficulty would appear to have afflicted his ethical theory, though it was a very different kind of difficulty from that which bothered the utilitarians. For, not being able to appeal to the facts of human life and human existence in support of his ethics, Kant could do little more than fall back upon the purely formal features of our moral concepts and moral discourse. The only trouble was: How could these forms be shown to have any application to the concrete content of human life and conduct?

But now, in the desire-and-duty ethic that has come to be so fashionable in the present day, are not these epistemological difficulties of both utilitarian and Kantian ethics quite successfully obviated? Thus as regards our human feelings and desires, it is not being claimed that there is anything moral or immoral about them just as such. Moral considerations become pertinent and relevant only when, having a desire to do just as I please, I then go on to say that I have a right to do so; or when, feeling a hatred toward my Jewish neighbors, I then move to the judgment that they ought to be exterminated. Moreover—and this is where the Kantian difficulties are outflanked—these moral considerations do indeed become relevant, and the formal features of moral discourse find their application and take on content. For the fact simply is that our desires, sentiments, and feelings about people and things do prompt us to make judgments about these same people and things—judgments of approval or disapproval, of praise or condemnation. And thus the logic of moral discourse comes into play, and morality itself is from then on firmly established.

In other words, Kant's difficulties with an excessive formalism apparently turn out to be just as gratuitous as the utilitarians' difficulties over not being able to find any formal moral structure in our desires at all. Moreover, both of these epistemological difficulties would appear to have been obviated without recourse to anything like natural law, or any sort of supposed ontological basis for ethics in nature or in reality. The mere logic of moral discourse suffices to provide an epistemology of morals without any ontology at all. What more could anyone want or ask for!

The Basic Weakness of the
New-Found Desire-and-Duty-Ethic

There is, though, a serious weakness in this currently fashionable desire-and-duty-ethic, if we may so term it. Moreover, the weakness would seem to be in the very foundations of the entire ethical-theoretical superstructure. Consider that very point of imposition at which the entire intricate scheme of moral concepts and moral rules, with all that they formally imply, is thought to be set down upon the manifold of our human desires and inclinations. Just how is this imposition effected? Unless we are much mistaken, it is on this very score that Hare and other contemporary writers have remained strangely silent.

If we go back to our own previous analysis of the nature and character of human desire, it can quickly be seen that this imposition is indeed a real problem. Desires, we noted, may be of two kinds, either reasoned or unreasoned. As a sort of paradigm of an unreasoned desire, precisely in the sense of a desire for which a reason would seem somehow irrelevant, was the example of someone's liking for spinach: "Why do you like spinach?" "Well, I don't know why, I just like it, that's all." Moreover, we remarked that the obvious impertinence of anything like reasons to desires of such a sort certainly does not mean that such desires are without causes.

However, it must not be thought that these unreasoned desires are necessarily restricted to trivial cases like a desire for spinach. Often desires of a much more sophisticated sort are those for which we may claim that no reasons of any kind are relevant or can be given. Thus it will be remembered that, in *The Merchant of Venice,* when Shylock is pressed by the Duke to explain why he insists upon his bond and will accept no substitute of any kind—not three thousand ducats, not the good will of his fellow Venetians, not the satisfaction of having tempered justice with mercy, nothing save that pound of flesh from Antonio's heart—he replies:

> . . . You'll ask me, why I rather choose to have
> A weight of carrion-flesh than to receive

Three thousand ducats: I'll not answer that:
But say, it is my humour; is it answer'd?
What if my house be troubl'd with a rat,
And I be pleas'd to give ten thousand ducats
To have it ban'd! What, are you answer'd yet?
Some men there are love not a gaping pig;
Some, that are mad if they behold a cat;
And others, when the bag-pipe sings i' the nose,
Masters of passion sways it to the mood
Of what it likes or loathes. Now, for your answer:
As there is not firm reason to be render'd,
Why he cannot abide a gaping pig;
Why he, a harmless necessary cat;
Why he, a woollen bag-pipe, but of force
Must yield to such inevitable shame
As to offend, himself being offended;
So can I give no reason, nor I will not,
More than a lodg'd hate and a certain loathing
I bear Antonio, that I follow thus
A losing suit against him. Are answer'd?
                                    [IV, 1, 40–61]

In this particular case Shylock's insistence on the irrelevance of reasons to what he wants to do may be nothing more than a pretense or perhaps even a rationalization for his own refusal to give reasons, knowing as he does that his real reasons are hatred of Christians in general and of Antonio in particular, and that these reasons are not good reasons or properly defensible reasons even in his own eyes.

But whether it is sometimes by way of mere pretense or not, the fact remains that our human desires and wishes and inclinations are often quite unreasoned and unreasoning. Moreover, when it comes to our instant question as to how in a desire-and-duty-ethic one is to understand the imposition of moral concepts upon desires, it must be carefully borne in mind that in such a context desires cannot be understood as being anything but unreasoned desires. We have already seen that for a desire to be a reasoned desire, the very logic of the situation requires that appeal be made to some good or value that is independent of the desire that is being justified or for which a reason is being sought. Thus, for instance, if I do try to give a reason for my wanting some spinach, I might say that the reason I want it is because I have found spinach to be good for me, it puts iron in my blood, or what not. Clearly, though, in such a case it is not because I want the spinach that I think it good for me, but rather the other way around. In fact, if the only reason I thought it good for me was the fact that I liked it, then I could hardly adduce its goodness as the reason for my liking it. And so one can see that what is involved here is but the old principle of a thing's being desired because it is good, rather than good because desired. Moreover, whenever it is a question of giving a reason for a desire, this very supposition that a reason might be relevant carries with it a presupposition as to the priority and independence of the goodness with respect to the desire which such goodness is being used to justify.

Nevertheless, we found it to be characteristic of any desire-ethic to hold that goodness is never thus really objective, such that the goodness could serve as the ground of the desire rather than the other way around. Accordingly, since it is just such a desire-ethic that is an integral part of what we have called the new desire-and-duty ethic, it is essential that in the context of such an ethic all desires are considered to be ultimately and in principle unreasoned desires. Otherwise, it would be necessary to ascribe to goodness and rightness, and indeed to all other moral or value properties of things, an independent ontological status in those things themselves, quite apart from how we feel about them. But this would go counter to the entire thrust and purpose of such an ethic.

Accordingly, then, it must be desires, considered as radically and ultimately unreasoned, that in the new ethic are held to be open to the imposition of moral notions and moral judgments upon them. But how?

Again going back to our earlier example drawn from Hare, we saw how it isn't enough for the Nazi merely to dislike his Jewish neighbors or even to want to have them exterminated. In addition, he must go on to make a moral judgment to the effect that they ought to be exterminated, or that it is right to exterminate them. Only when such a judgment is made, whether explicitly or implicitly, and not until then, can Hare's entire apparatus of the logic of moral notions get off the ground, so to speak. To be sure, once this initial moral judgment is made, then Hare can show how it is universalizable, and that in being universalized it must carry with it implications, which hopefully the Nazi would be quite unwilling to accept and as a result of which he would come to repudiate his own original judgment. But where does this initial judgment come from? What possible justification is there for it? How can a mere unreasoned sentiment of dislike or hatred of Jews be turned into a moral judgment of condemnation?

Or consider again that other somewhat more sketchy example with reference to Singer's generalization principle. The point of that example was that I might have an inclination simply to do what I want, to go my own way, to do as I please. What Singer then wanted to show was that by virtue of the generalization principle, even such a natural and idle inclination on my part must nevertheless implicate me in a whole set of obligations and counter-obligations with respect to my fellow man. Still, there is no way in which Singer's generalization principle can possibly be brought to bear on my inclination, until that inclination is either explicitly or implicitly converted into a moral judgment to the effect that I have a right to do as I please. Then, and not till then, does all that elaborate machinery of the logic of moral notions come into play. Accordingly, the question again becomes one as to just how from an admittedly unreasoned desire a moral judgment could even arise to begin with.

The question is more than just a passing one, for the thing whose very possibility is being asked about is indeed an utter impossibility. We have already noted how Kant made the point quite decisively, although not in these very terms, that no desire or inclination could ever be the basis for a moral law, simply because a desire—and by that he meant an unreasoned desire, since he recognized no other kind—was something for which ultimately no reason could be given and which therefore was not susceptible of such universality as was requisite for any properly moral law. That, indeed, was really the substance of Kant's entire attack on any and all forms of a desire-ethic.

But, you will retort, this is surely a very farfetched criticism, if not one that is downright wrongheaded. For whatever either Kant or any natural-law theorist might say to the contrary, the fact is that over and over again, and just as a matter of fact, human beings do tend to convert what they feel strongly about, or even more generally the ordinary pro- or con-attitudes that they have toward things, into moral judgments. Indeed,

Hare might say that that is just what so many Nazis did: they converted their unreasoned, though not necessarily uncaused, hatred of the Jews into judgments having moral import, such as that the Jews ought to be exterminated. And that, Hare might say, is just what he was bent on criticizing and attacking, this uncritical slide from mere feelings to moral judgments.

Yet, strictly speaking, this is not what Hare was criticizing or attacking at all. In fact, nowhere does he have any criticism to make of our feelings and desires just as such. Or, in case there are places that we have overlooked where Hare does hazard such criticisms, perhaps we ought to guard ourselves by saying that on Hare's own principles it would hardly seem that he could consistently be critical of any mere feelings that anyone might happen to have, whether of hatred of the Jews or of indifference to human suffering or what. Nor does Hare criticize that admittedly inveterate tendency which all of us human beings have to convert our sentiments, our desires, our pro- and con-attitudes, into moral judgments. Thus Hare would surely acknowledge that there is nothing either wrong or mistaken about someone's proceeding from "I don't like x" to "x is bad," or "I don't like what a is doing" to "What a is doing is wrong." It is only after the judgment has been made, and after it has been universalized, that one begins to see that one's judgment is fraught with implications that one either cannot or is unwilling to accept; it is then and only then that one faults one's original judgment; but it is never faulted for having been the result of an illicit process from mere feeling to moral judgment.

The same point might be confirmed in terms of the example which we considered with reference to Singer. When I say that something is all right for me to do, simply because I want to do it, the error does not lie in this inference. Instead, it is only when by the generalization principle I see that, if what I wanted to do is all right for me, it must be all right for anyone else to do; and then further, when by the generalization argument I come to see that if everyone were to do what I want to do, the consequences would be disastrous (or at least undesirable)—it is only then that I come to recognize that there is something faulty in my original judgment to the effect that it is perfectly all right for me to do the particular thing that I wanted to do. Indeed, in characteristic utilitarian fashion, neither that initial judgment nor my initial action (supposing that I went ahead and acted on my judgment) is held to be wrong just as such, but only because of the consequences.

Accordingly, our criticism of this entire contemporary enterprise of a desire-and-duty ethic is that it rests on shaky foundations. For the entire machinery of the logic of moral discourse which is supposed to enable us effectively either to approve or condemn our actions simply on the basis of their consequences cannot even be set in motion until certain initial moral judgments have been made for which there is not the slightest warrant or basis, either moral or logical.

It may be objected that such a criticism of the contemporary desire-and-duty ethic is surely off base. Why is it not possible to bring a properly critical judgment to bear on those processes and transitions that we make from pro- or con-attitudes to moral judgments? Indeed, might it not be possible to legitimate these transitions in some cases, and then why might not the logic of moral discourse, which would appear to be so beloved by so many contemporary linguistic philosophers, take off from there? For instance, what of the following simple examples? Suppose that I feel suspicious of someone with whom I have had dealings, and just don't like him. Still, I have no real reasons for my suspicions and dislikes, and hence I carefully refrain from making any judgment in condemnation of the man. Imagine, though, that later I come across some evidence that definitely confirms my suspicions and justifies my dislike, so that now I feel I can make some moral judgments in the way of criticism and censure. Would this not be an entirely legitimate process from feeling to judgment?

Or take the example that we have so often employed with reference to Singer and his generalization principle. For what, after all, is wrong with my sometimes doing just what I like, for no particular reason other than that I am tired and want to enjoy myself, and that what I want to indulge myself in—say, an afternoon of fishing—would presumably be of no particular harm to man or beast,[34] myself included!

What is interesting about these examples is that both of them involve not simply the conversion of mere feelings and desires into moral judg-

---

34. No, not even to the fish, given my customary no-luck.

ments, but rather the conversion of unreasoned desires into reasoned ones. Thus in the first case, my dislike of the man, which was originally a dislike for which I had no reason—"I don't know why I disliked him; I just do"—becomes a reasoned dislike. I now dislike the man because of certain real shortcomings in him which I have since learned about and which can serve as proper reasons for my dislike. Or, in the other example, of course there may be very good reasons for my wanting to indulge myself in some idle pastime: it might be simply the reason that I need rest and relaxation for my health and well-being. But then my desire to do just what I want for a change would no longer be an unreasoned desire, but rather one for which I can give quite good reasons.

However, as soon as those desires which serve as the basis for certain of our initial moral judgments turn out to be reasoned desires, then we have left the domain of a desire-ethic in any and all of its forms. For all reasoned desires presuppose a situation in which things are desired because they are good, rather than good merely because desired; and this situation, in turn, invokes an entire ethical setting in which goodness and value have an objective, ontological status in things and in the world, as opposed to a setting where goodness and value owe their existence entirely to us and to the feelings and desires that we have for things. Apparently, then, that popular contemporary version of a desire-ethic—according to which we are entirely free in the matter of our preferences and evaluations, the only restriction on the latter being due to our rational recognition of the implications of our moral discourse—cannot properly and legitimately even so much as get off the ground. Either those initial and particular moral judgments that are determined by our feelings and inclinations, and that are presupposed in all efforts to trace out the implications of our moral language, are quite baseless and unwarranted; or they are warranted, inasmuch as our feelings and desires are reasoned desires. In the former case, the mere formal implications of the terms of our moral discourse would seem to be irrelevant. In the latter case, the formal logic of moral discourse, while certainly not irrelevant, is definitely secondary, for the real sources of our rational moral judgments lie not in the formal implications of the moral and ethical terms that we use, but rather in the facts of nature and of ourselves.

Apparently, then, Kant was right after all: a desire-ethic, no matter how hard it may try, can never really manage to generate an ethics at all. Moreover, the ingenious contemporary undertaking simply to impose upon a desire-ethic all of those implications that Kant saw to be formally involved in the use of moral notions just doesn't come off, and the pretended imposition proves to be really no more than an imposture. It is true that by picking up the threads of arguments developed in earlier chapters we can find other things wrong with this currently fashionable utilitarianism in Kantian dress. For one thing, in order to show that men cannot possibly avoid the language of morals and the logic of moral discourse, even though there is no sort of ontology of morals to provide the language and the logic with a proper ground and justification, recourse must be had to the transcendental turn in one of its various forms and manifestations. The disabilities of this device as a means of saving ethics from nihilism we have already reviewed and commented on.

For another thing, this new utilitarian program, as it is pushed by thinkers like Hare and Singer, would seem to suffer from much the same standard difficulty that has always afflicted utilitarianism: just how all of the desires, interests, pleasures, etc., that must be reckoned with in tracing out the consequences of any action can ever be intelligibly reckoned in and reckoned with so as to be properly reconciled or maximized or synthesized or what have you. To take Singer as a case in point, we have seen how he formulates his generalization argument: "If everyone were to do x, the consequences would be disastrous (or undesirable); therefore no one ought to do x." Yet he offers no criterion at all for determining what constitutes the disastrous in such cases. As for the notion of the undesirable or the desirable, doubtless he would follow Mill and say that the best way to determine what is desirable would be to learn what is desired. But alas, desires are notoriously fickle and whimsical both in individuals and in mankind as a whole. What, then, must our criterion for the desirable be—what the deltas and others of *Brave New World* hold to be desirable, or what a Plato or an Aristotle might teach is truly desirable?

Moreover, we must confess that Hare's ingenious device for universalizing our moral judgments so as to determine whether we ourselves might be willing to accept all of the consequences seems hardly as unequivocal in its import as one might like. It is hard to imagine any moral judgment which when universalized could not be seen to have implications which would be disagreeable and profoundly upsetting to some people. Very well, then, if the one who originally propounded the judgment were to imaginatively put himself in the shoes of such unfortunates, would this mean that he would then feel he needed to surrender his own original judgment? But then how could any moral judgment hope to survive?

However, all such difficulties connected with the current desire-and-duty ethic—that it cannot avoid having recourse to the transcendental turn, and that it has no proper criterion for distinguishing acceptable from unacceptable consequences of our decisions and actions—we can perhaps consider secondary to the more fundamental one, which is that its attempted superimposition of duties upon desires simply fails, with the result that the whole superstructure of this elaborate ethical theory turns out to have no foundation at all.

Conclusion:

Back to an Ontology of Morals!

If the dilemmas of utilitarianism and Kantianism have not been resolved by the partisans of a desire-and-duty-ethic, why not conclude that the sensible course is to make a clean break with all of these varied attempts to have an ethics without ontology? After all, we have suggested that the fundamental reason for Kant's not being able to extricate himself from his formalism was that he failed to see that although any ethics which sought to make goodness dependent upon desire was no ethics at all, this did not necessarily preclude the possibility that human desires might well be reasoned desires after all. In that case, the business of ethics might simply be one of trying to get men to desire what was really good. Likewise, we would hope that we had thoroughly scotched that old Moorean snake of the indefinability of goodness and of the supposed logical impossibility of ever being able to equate goodness with any of the real features or properties of things in the world. In short, is not the way clear—at least the logical way—to a return to something like an ontology of morals once again? Indeed, how else can the epistemological difficulties of an ethical knowledge be successfully resolved, and the impending threat of an ethical nihilism averted?

INDEX